From Catholic School Rooms to Radicalised Student Movement

Edited by Hilary D Regan

From Catholic School Rooms to Radicalised Student Movement

The Australian YCS in the 60s, 70s and early 80's

Edited by Hilary D Regan

Adelaide
2023

Text copyright ©2023 remains the individual authors and ATF Press for the collection. All rights reserved. Except for any fair dealing under the Copyright Act, no part of the publication may be reproduced by any means without prior permission. Inquiries should be made in the first instance with the publisher.

Cover Design: Myf Cadwallader

Cardijn Studies: On the Church in the World of Today
Volume 4, Number 1, 2023

The *Cardijn Studies* journal is a refereed journal which aims to document the history of the Jocist, Cardijn inspired, lay movements both historically and in the present day as well as the examining the rich tradition of Catholic Social teaching on the Church in the world of today. Articles cover a range of areas: the spirituality, methodology and the history of these traditions and movements in the Church and in society.

Editor: Hilary Dominic Regan

Editorial Board

- **Assistant Professor Kevin Ahern**, Manhattan College, New York, USA.
- **Dr Ana Maria Bidegain**, Professor of Latin American Religions at Florida International University, USA.
- **Fr Michael Deeb OP**, former IYCS Chaplain South Africa
- **David Moloney**, professional historian, Cardijn Community Australia executive member
- **Stefan Gigacz**, Secretary Cardijn Community, Australia

Business Manager, Editor and Publisher:
Mr Hilary Dominic Regan, ATF Press Publishing Group, PO Box 234, Brompton, SA 5007, Australia.
Email: hdregan@atf.org.au

ISBN		
	978-1-923006-20-1	soft
	978-1-923006-21-8	hard
	978-1-923006-22-5	epub
	978-1-923006-23-2	pdf

Published and edited by

Making a lasting impact

An imprint of the ATF Press Publishing Group
owned by ATF (Australia) Ltd.
PO Box 234
Brompton, SA 5007
Australia
ABN 90 116 359 963
www.atfpress.com
Making a lasting impact

Cardijn Studies: On the Church in the World of Today: Volume 4/1 2023

Table of Contents

Editorial ix
    Hilary D Regan

1. The Young Christian Students Movement in the 1960s and its Response to Vatican II 1
    Brian Lawrence

2. YCS Regional Work, Ballarat and Sandhurst Dioceses; 1971–1972 27
    Trevor Bate

3. YCS in the 1970s 35
    Carmel Brown

4. YCS in Adelaide from 1974–1975 45
    Catherine Whewell

5. 'Like a Bird on the Wire': One Experience of Australian YCS in the Exciting, Tumultuous 1970s 57
    Pat Walsh

6. YCS in the 1970s and 1980s 81
    Linda Baker

7. The Student Movement and the YCS in the Early 1970s 93
    Mark Considine and Anthony J Regan

Biographical details of the contributors 109

Cardijn Studies: On the Church in the World of Today: Volume 4/1 2023

From Catholic School Rooms to Radicalised Student Movement
The Australian YCS in the 60s, 70s and early 80's

The image on the front of this publication comes from a document put together in 1992 to mark the fiftieth anniversary of the founding of the YCS (Young Christian Students) movement in Australia. The image of young Catholic school-girls on the cover of the publication is key to understanding the history of the Australian YCS.

The YCS was first introduced into Australia in 1942 and was essentially for many years Catholic school-based, with resources and programs sent to groups in schools from the National Office. While the National Executive had some student representation on it for some time, it became much more of a student led movement, a movement for students, by students (to paraphrase Cardijn) in the late 1960s and early 1970s.

For many years prior it was a top-down organisation, coming from the Catholic bishops, through the National Secretariat for Catholic Action, and where the YCS existed it essentially was run by religious and priests in those Catholic schools.[1] In 1961 the first National YCS Conference was held in Melbourne, Victoria, with student representatives, as well as religious, priests and at least one bishop (Bishop James Glesson as he then was), with those who attended coming from twelve dioceses around the country. The early national conferences (1961, 1964 and 1968) were organised by the National Office (as were the thousands of national programs sent to groups each February[2]), which included National Chaplain, Fr Paul Kane, who was involved

---

1. In 1964 the first groups began in 'state schools'.
2. Fr Kane, taken from the 1992 50th anniversary history document published by the YCS.

with YCS for many years.[3] In 1967 Marlene Dunn Fr Kane and Fr Kevin Murphy represented the Australian YCS for the first time at an international meeting in Canada.

Records show that by 1963 there were 446 active groups and 25,000 members in Australia.[4] The 1960's saw the start of a what was to be later termed a 'National Team' of student leaders, full-time workers.[5] Brian Lawrence, contributor to this volume, worked with Marlene Dunn (1962 to 1969) from 1968 to 1969 in Melbourne, the home of the National YCS. In the late 1960s and early 1970s saw full-time workers appointed in various dioceses to work alongside and with the National Team in the new directions the YCS was taking. Some of these people are contributors to this volume.

For many in Australia and elsewhere the 1960s and 1970s were a period of massive change. The period after the Second World War in Australia was the time of the so-called the 'baby-boomers'. It was a period in which global events of radical action such as the Paris riots of 1968 began to ripple around the world, including Australia. It was a time when people became more aware of, and protested against, oppressive military regimes in South America, Asia (and the Vietnam War in particular) and of apartheid in South Africa. It was the beginning of the sexual revolution. There was an upheaval in many families as young people began to question all forms of authority.

In the Catholic Church Vatican II saw many changes in the Church, as it generally became more outward looking in various of its documents. One cannot ignore the importance of the impact of the Catholic Church's long tradition of Catholic Social teachings going back to Pope Leo's encyclical *Rerum Novarum*, of 1891, to Pope John XXIII's 1961 encyclical *Mater et Magistra*, in what was happening to the YCS all groups in the Church concerned with 'social issues'.

The Council documents and the Church's tradition of Social Teachings were significant intellectual theological documents that

---

3. Fr Paul Kane started as Chaplain in Melbourne in 1955 and became part-time National Chaplain in 1961 and was full-time from 1968 to 1971. Taken from the 1992 50th anniversary history document published by the YCS.
4. Taken from the 1992 50th anniversary history document published by the YCS.
5. In 1968 elections were held for the first time of President and Secretary. Marlene Dunn was elected National President and Brian Lawrence as National Secretary. Till then the National Executive had some student representation. Over time that increased.

supported, gave a framework and one could possibly argue led to some extent a radicalisation in thinking. Undoubtedly both became part of the 'mix' in the factors that led to a move towards a more radicalised focus of the leadership of the YCS movement in Australia which gathered pace from the late 1960s.

The post Vatican II era was also the beginning of a fall in religious and priestly vocations all over the world.

Later, in the 1970s, also saw the beginning of a steady decline of many young people going to Mass which has continued through to today with few Catholic young people attending Mass.

Young people in the Catholic school system, joined a local YCS group in their senior years for a variety of reasons. For some it replaced or added to their 'Religious Education', program, or was just one of the different groups one could join at the school, were encouraged to do so by a nun or priest at the school, or was that group one tended to drift into for no particular reason other than they were not part of the sporting types at the school. YCS groups were commonplace in many Catholic schools around the country at the time and were often led, or were 'assisted', by the nuns, brothers or priests in the school. Groups would vary from school to school in what they did and often there was little connection within the city or diocese between the different groups. Sometimes the involvement by adults was more directive, while at other times less so leaving it up to the students to run the group. The direction/involvement of the priest or religious depended often on the interest of the adult 'assistant' or chaplain and how important it was for them in what was often an already heavy workload within the school.

This collection of essays has been written by those who were involved in the secondary YCS in Australia in the 1960s, 1970s and 1980s either at state, diocesan, regional or national level. It documents the changes that were occurring in the YCS in that period. Those changes were one's which reflected to a certain extent what was happening in society and within the Catholic Church. The movement was changing from being essentially Catholic school—based groups, with a national chaplain, to being a national movement led by student leaders for students.[6]

---

6. For more detail on this change see *New Visions of Priesting, Cardijn Studies*, 3 (2022): 46–52.

It was a period of radicalisation where there was for many in the Catholic Church hierarchy, nuns, priests, brothers and bishops, a discomfort with what they saw as a 'new' direction that was being taken by the student leaders in an organisation which they had known and, often, nurtured and seen grow, and which they were, until then, comfortable with. In the early 1970s, in a number of cities around the country the YCS was supported financially by the local diocese with a paid full-time worker and office space provided.

The YCS was a 'known' and 'accepted' part of the school life and religious or priests took on being assistants as part of their work at the school. Now that world was changing. Many of the chaplains, assistants and bishops, but not all, did not have a framework to understand what was happening to a movement they themselves had often grown up with and been part of.

In the late 1960s and early 1970s student leaders who were in their late teens were questioning everything including the involvement of priests and nuns in the movement and asking searching theological questions about the role of priests in the movement. The student leaders were asking what for some priests and religious were challenging questions, questions of what had been the basis of Catholic theology for many hundreds of years. For example, what was uniqueness of the priesthood within Catholicism, of the long-standing belief of an ontological difference between priests and lay people? Some student leaders in the early 1970s would raise this at national meetings and refer to it as being the 'X' factor. Frictions and tensions often arose in those meetings.

As Bob Wilkinson recalls 'the student leaders were more interested in authenticity than in preserving the near three decades of Catholic school YCS, a pride of Catholic education'.[7]

Differences emerged as well with the bishops. One example of the differences that emerged was a decision taken by national leaders in the mid 1970s not to accept an invitation from the bishops to participate in a youth Mass during a Eucharistic Congress in Melbourne.[8]

Wilkinson writes 'One of the bishops I met asked me, "What is happening to the Young people, Bob?". He was referring specifically to the YCS whose leaders were paid by the bishops . . . this docile student organisation had been a model of faithful Catholic youth.'[9]

---

7. See *New Visions of Priesting*, 49.
8. See *New Visions of Priesting*, 48.
9. See *New Visions of Priesting*, 48.

Students leaders, and full-time workers (normally full-timers were straight out of school themselves), were, by the early late 1960s and early 1970s, increasingly taking on more and more of the leadership roles at the local, diocesan and national levels.

Attendance at international events at a regional, Asian, level or later at world meetings, and contact by visits from leaders of the YCS from other parts of the world, had an influence in the thinking and actions of full-time workers and leaders in Australia. Prior to this local groups began to be led by students and the role of religious and priests was being questioned at national meetings and by the leaders. Changes were occurring at many levels. Groups began to use new programs and material from the national office, which had a more politically based focus, examining the 'signs of the times', looking at injustices and oppressive political regimes around the world, using social and political analysis to study the world, and generally developing a more 'outward looking' focus than earlier times. Groups were visited by full-time workers bringing in new insights of the role of the YCS and its structure. For may this was challenging. The see-judge-act model, the 'review of life method', was not just a manner of personal reflection of 'good acts' but was developed as a method of looking at the whole of one's life with many taking on a different view of their Christian vocation, a movement of students which was seen as being part of larger movements changing the world.

On the one hand, this was the period of radical change within the leadership due to their connections with international events, attendance at overseas meetings and visits by international leaders. And on the other hand, it saw the collapse, closing-down and disappearance of many of the Catholic school-based groups around the country. Few schools would now, by the mid 1970s, have groups which students could join as often had occurred in the past.

The YCS in Australia quite quickly then became a movement with a much smaller base with fewer groups in many places. Those who had been leaders in the schools were now leaders of the movement at a national level or had moved on. The chaplains and assistants from the past had now also moved on, retired, left the priesthood or religious life, or for some, though not all, they no longer understood the 'new' focus and direction of the YCS. A small number of religious and priests did understand and or accepted where the movement was going, supported the leadership and remained involved. However, the decline of numbers of groups and individuals continued and was mirrored in a lack of Mass attendance by many young people. That decline in Mass attendance continues today despite large numbers of people attending Catholic schools around the country.

Today, in 2023, there would be very few school-based groups, with a presence in only a few dioceses, and only a handful of members and groups around the country. Only a few dioceses around the country today support the YCS financially and now often money is spent on a wider focussed youth ministry office and programs within many dioceses with a stronger presence of chaplains and adult assistants. At the same time, there are some places in Australia where now the YCS and YCW are more or less combined into one body with no specialised separation between workers and students. Finances are an issue especially when the bishops, with rare exceptions, do not contribute financially.

This volume of essays then is a documentation of the period of the 1960s, 1970s ad early 1980s by some of those who were involved in this period of change in Australia. It should be noted that what was occurring in the YCS was also mirrored in many ways with the Australian YCW (Young Christian Workers).[10]

This is a project that has taken some time to assemble and was first suggested four years ago. ATF Press is grateful to those who have taken the time to cast their minds back some forty or fifty more years to reflect on that period and their involvement with the YCS and to write about those times. Some who were approached declined as their memories of evets so long ago would not, in their view, be sufficient to provide any great detail. Many things have happened in between and it is not always easy to remember with great clarity events from so long ago. For some who accepted to write doing so brought details and memories than what they originally thought would be the case. Thus, over time this volume has come together with various drafts along the way. No doubt, as with all historical publications, some may differ with some of the details, exact dates, timing, sequences and locations contained in the articles that follow.

This volume of memories, reflections and recollections is not intended to be a comprehensive or detailed history of the YCS in Australia during this period. That would be another task well beyond what the scope of what was envisaged when this project was suggested

---

10. *New Visions of Priesting*, 46–47.

and would require examining minutes of meetings, summaries of national councils, conferences and have additional contributors. It is, rather, the memories of a small number of people who were involved as full-time workers with the YCS in various places, who held different positions, who were invited to write and who agreed to recall and write about what they knew about the YCS in the late 1960s through to the early 1980s.

Memories may differ on exact details as to what happened or who did or said what, but there is a common view within the pieces that follow that this period saw much change in the YCS. It changed from what had been a school-based grouping of students, to some extent inwardly focused, led by adults around the country to what became a radicalised student led movement with more of an outward focus questioning all and everything.

To a large degree the YCS movement everywhere, locally and internationally, became a much smaller body and nothing has ever really replaced it, not one that brings all the elements of the Cardijn inspired movements of action and reflection, and student leadership such as was the history of the YCS in the Catholic Church. That is, there is no action-reflection-action model, no student led body for students that is part of a network of small group of reflection that fits within a larger network of groups, locally and internationally, with a common vision. Groups concerned with broad based social justice issues in schools which have developed in some places, and often as part of the schools Religious Education program, is only the starting point of a student led movement for students such as the YCS.

It has been an important task to document in written form the events of the 1960s through to the early 1980s by those involved, otherwise the history and knowledge of the events could be lost. This volume adds to and continues on from the previous edition of *Cardijn Studies*, Volume 3, 2022,[11] which has the interview with Fr Bob Wilkinson, of Adelaide, and referred to in this collection. He has been a significant contributor to many of the lay movements within the Catholic Church in Australia.

Hilary D Regan
March 2023

---

11. *New Visions of Priesting.*

The Young Christian Students Movement in the 1960s and its Response to Vatican II

Brian Lawrence

Asking someone to write about the events of their youth, as I have been asked to do for this series, is an invitation to the writer to reflect on their 'coming-of-age' years. There is a danger in reflecting on these years of seeing them as pivotal years in the nation's history, or in Church history, rather than seeing those years as a snapshot of longer-term trends. There is a risk that the reflections may be too subjective. Nevertheless, these coming-of-age years may coincide with a time of momentous change, such as the changes wrought by the Covid Pandemic. I am inclined to the view that the 1950s to the 1970s should be seen as a continuum, even though there were significant markers within that time, such as the student riots in Europe in 1968 and the emergence and impact of opposition to the Vietnam War. Some of this change was driven by the emergence of youth as a significant social and economic class.

The life of the youth movements of the Catholic Church, and the Young Christian Students (YCS) in particular, cannot be disengaged from these broader social changes. But for the YCS, like for Catholics generally, the 1960s was a period of great change, with a leap greater than any change in society generally. Two aspects stand out: the impact of Pope John XXIII, now sainted, and the reforms of the Second Vatican Council (Vatican II) that he initiated. Vatican II was intended to 'open the windows and let in some fresh air'. It did.

In setting the scene for the YCS in the late 1960s, a few words on my own experience could illustrate changes in the Church. In 1956 I was a ten-year old altar boy reciting responses in Latin in a church where the priest had his back to the congregation during the most important part of the Mass, when only altar boys could just see what he was doing. For me, there were things to do: lighting and snuffing out candles, mumbling the Latin responses, presenting the cruets of water and wine, remembering to ring the bells at the right time, and holding the communion-plate under the chins of those kneeling at the altar rail to receive communion. But for those on the other side of the altar rail there was little physical engagement. It seemed to have always been so.

Ten years later, with Vatican II finished in December 1965, the documents of the Council had opened the Church to thinking that had been developing within the Church, but which was unexpected by most Catholics. It is sometimes overlooked that Pope John XXIII's social encyclicals *Mater et Magistra* (1961) and *Pacem in Terris* (1963) had started to shape the way in which many Catholics viewed their role in secular affairs.

For most Catholics Vatican II manifested itself in the changes to the Mass. Latin was gone and the priest faced the congregation and spoke in English. That was momentous enough, but it also carried opportunities for lay participation and, especially, youth participation. Prayers of the Faithfull and Offertory Processions gave them an opportunity to express their faith. 'Youth' and 'Folk' masses featuring hymns sung in English, reflecting some contemporary musical styles, were popular. Para-liturgies were also developed by and for students and youth in schools and parishes. These new and challenging activities drew many into an active social circle which was part of the strength of Church youth activities in the 1960s. And this was a time when most young Catholics attended Sunday Mass.

But there was something more profound going on. From the late 1930s there had been increased interest in the lay apostolate and, in particular, the Catholic Action movements in Europe. The Archbishop of Melbourne, Daniel Mannix, was a strong supporter of new lay movements. Consider the following report in *The Advocate* (published by the Archdiocese of Melbourne) of 7 November 1945 regarding a speech given by the Archbishop to a meeting of some 350 YCS members, under the heading 'Laity Should Lead in Catholic Action'. The introduction stated that the Archbishop had delivered an 'important pronouncement on the respective roles of clergy and laity in Catholic Action':

"It was most heartening and inspiring for him to find himself in the midst of young people, said his Grace the Archbishop, addressing the gathering of young students during the afternoon. He felt, at the end of a long life [he was 81 and lived for another 18 years], that he had lived into a new era, because he could well remember the time when anything like that gathering would be quite unthinkable. Catholics in Australia and elsewhere were always good religious people; but sometimes the more religious they were the more they kept to themselves and the less help they were prepared to give to others. Their idea was that they had come into the world to save their own souls and they looked upon that as a full-time employment.

With modern conditions that theory had been exploded, said his Grace. One of the most remarkable things done by any of the Popes—and very remarkable men in recent times they had been—was when Pius XI started this great movement of Catholic Action . . .

It enabled the modem Catholic world to change its outlook, and to attempt things, and achieve them, that would have been quite impossible before Pius XI touched this spiritual button and set going the new spiritual machinery.

This movement, as an organised movement, was quite a new thing in the Church . . . He had a feeling sometimes that in some places there might be difficulty in changing over. The laity might still be inclined to rely too much and too heavily upon the priests; and the priests, too, might be inclined to take a place within the Catholic Action movement that the Pope never intended. But in Catholic Action it was fundamental that the leaders were to be lay people, young and old: the priest had his place not as leader, but rather as a sort of trusted consultor, who would be ready to give his advice when it was needed.

In Australia, he believed they were giving an example of Catholic Action at its best, said the Archbishop. He did not know any place where Catholic Action had made more progress than in Australia, and he hoped that the lay people would continue to take their proper place in the movement, and, if necessary, insist on their right, to leadership and initiative.

> Nobody could challenge their right. The priests, on their side, would walk warily, and be ready to foresee difficulties and in due time give sound and wise advice whenever it might be needed. It was not the Pope's intention, nor was it needful, that they should lead the various movements. Their work was to guide gently and cautiously the activities started and. worked out by the laity." (Subheadings omitted.)
> https://trove.nla.gov.au/newspaper/article/172223806

This is a remarkable passage, well in advance of Vatican II's recognition of the right of the laity to participate in the mission of the Church. In Melbourne, at least, this attitude had permeated the lay movements, though by Vatican II the use of the term Catholic Action had mostly fallen into disuse. The term Catholic Action was emerging in political debate in connection with the campaigns by Catholics to counter the influence of communists in the trade union movement and to strengthen their influence in the Australian Labor Party.

In addressing a YCS rally in May 1950 Archbishop Mannix said:

> I am sorry we ever called this work Catholic Action—the name was being used in other places before the movement reached Australia—a name which is so frequently misunderstood. For many reasons, the title 'lay apostolate' would have been much better. https://trove.nla.gov.au/newspaper/article/172511173

As best I can recall my time in the Young Christian Workers (YCW) and later working for the YCS, the term Catholic Action had no significant contemporary use in the 1960s. We were involved in the lay apostolate, the youth apostolate, or the student apostolate.

The YCS and the YCW were established by the bishops, but with the stated objective that they would be run by their members, by students and by young workers. No doubt, there were many instances of a failure to observe the demarcations stressed by Archbishop Mannix in 1945, but, overall, the YCS was run by students for students. And the YCW was run by young workers for young workers. Moreover, many of those members understood that they were the Catholic Church in action in their own vocations and spheres of influence. Of course, this was reinforced by commentaries coming out of Vatican II, particularly the *Decree on the Apostolate of the Laity* in December 1965, the last month of the Council.

It is important to appreciate that the YCW and the YCS were established in each diocese by a mandate from the local bishop. In Melbourne the YCW, from 1941, and the YCS, from 1942, were constituted as agencies of the Archdiocese and were part of the structure of the Archdiocese, the organisational link being diocesan chaplains appointed by the Archbishop. In this respect they were like the current day 'official' youth ministries of Australian dioceses.

In summary, this was the Church in which the YCS operated in the 1960s.

Before saying more, it is useful to remind ourselves that, at the present time, all Australian Catholics under the age of 25 have grown up in a Church beset by the scandal and devastations of sexual abuse within the Church. By contrast, the 1960s was a period when students and young workers could be enthusiastic about their Church, especially given the kinds of views expressed by Archbishop Mannix and Vatican II. Sure, there was some apathy in the 1960s, but we now have significant antipathy.

I have limited knowledge of the YCS in the early to mid-1960s. My knowledge of the youth apostolate came through the YCW, which I joined in Fawkner in 1960 when I turned fourteen, the school leaving age at the time. I did not move beyond parish sporting and social activities until my second year at Melbourne University. In the following two years I was very active in the 'apostolic' side of the YCW in the parish and at the university. In the parish we established a YCS group for secondary students and another group for tertiary students. The Diocesan Chaplain of the YCW (Fr Paul Willy) put me in touch with three YCW Branch Presidents (Peter Cowan, Bill O'Shea, and Darrel Bowyer) who were also at Melbourne University and the four of us started Jocist groups in the university. (The name being derived from the initials of Jeunesse Ouvrière Chrétienne, the French YCW.) We saw them as extensions of our YCW membership, but they were not YCW groups. These were different times without the pressures that are now on students. As well as being active in my parish, I was, for those two years, the Secretary of the Law Students' Society and involved in various SRC-related campus activities. When I finished Law School at the end of 1967, I got a job offer from the National Office of the YCS which was then based in Melbourne. I seemed to be a reasonable fit for the YCS's plans for parishes and tertiary education. I was National Secretary in 1968 and National President in 1969.

In the late 1960s the Melbourne YCW was strong in many parishes, well-organised by full time workers and backed by a large network of priests who were committed to the lay apostolate as expounded by Archbishop Mannix, Cardinal Joseph Cardijn (the founder of the YCW) and Vatican II. The enormous YCW football competition throughout Melbourne enabled YCW branches to stay connected with a wide range of youth in their parishes. In 1969 we had about 40 parish YCS groups and twenty or more parish tertiary student groups in Melbourne. Overall, there were about 5,000 students in the YCS, the vast majority in school groups.

My time with the YCS coincided with the start of a marked change in its 'membership'. I use that word loosely because at this time there was no formal membership and YCS numbers were estimated by the number of annual programmes, or handbooks, sold by the National Office. In 1968 more than 30,000 were sold. By the early 1970s the sales had fallen to less than 10,000. This was the start of a long decline in YCS numbers.

Space does not permit a discussion of the reasons for this initial decline, but it was, in my view, mostly caused by the emergence of what we called the 'New Catechetics' and the commercial publications that came with this change. The YCS and the YCS publications had become part of the Religious Education curriculum in many schools because of their ability to link faith and the lives and interests of students. That was the substance of the new catechetics and the publications it inspired were more professional in content and presentation than we could produce in the YCS. We consoled ourselves with the thought that it would only impact on 'book members'. We were wrong. One Melbourne girls' school which had YCS groups from the early days replaced the YCS with 'Catechetics'. On top of this, by the early 1970s the YCS had to cope with falling numbers of Religious Assistants in schools and priests in parishes.

Despite the threat from these changes, the YCS and the new catechetics shared a common theology and pedagogy. A key figure in post-Vatican II catechetics in Melbourne, and beyond, was Fr Tom Doyle, later Monsignor Tom Doyle AO, Chair of the National Catholic Education Commission. He became the Director of Religious Education in the Archdiocese when I was working for the YCS and was based in the building next to the YCS offices in Cathedral Hall. I had known him very well since my university days. Tom Doyle was the priest who had the greatest influence on me while I was at university and in my YCS years. With the help of Fr Frank Little, later the Archbishop of Melbourne, we were able to have him 'appointed' by the Archdiocese as the *de facto* chaplain to the National YCS workers during the substantial period between the official national appointments of Frs Paul Kane and Pat Walsh. Tom Doyle and three other priests, Frs Barry Moran, Eric Hodgens and Bob Maguire, were very well-known for their activities supporting tertiary students from the mid-1960s. The Chaplain's house at Ozanam House, where Tom and Eric lived, was like a clubhouse for many of us. The four priests, like many other young priests in the Archdiocese, were not only in sync with Vatican II, but were ahead of it in regard to the lay apostolate. For that we need to recognise the leadership of Archbishop Mannix, Archbishop Simonds, the Coadjutor Archbishop of Melbourne from 1942, and Fr Charles ('Charlie') Mayne SJ, Rector of archdiocesan seminaries from 1947 to 1968.

I should also make a necessarily brief reference to the political context in which the YCS worked. In the 1960s the Democratic Labour Party (DLP) continued to bleed votes away from the Australian Labour Party (ALP), as it had done since the mid-1950s when the DLP emerged from the ALP. The DLP was a predominantly Catholic party with its origins in differences over the role of Catholic Action movements, differing views on the threat that communists posed to Australian society and disputes about whether and how Catholics should organise in the ALP and trade unions. 'The Split' kept the ALP out of office federally and in those States, such as Victoria, where the DLP was strong. Many Catholic families, including my extended family, were split by the issue. Support for the DLP among Parish Priests and Religious was especially strong, but among curates the proportion was more even. Perhaps most YCS members came from DLP-supporting families, but there would not have been much in it.

The great achievement of the YCW in Melbourne (and in other places) was keeping party politics out of the YCW. There was a still plenty of scope for social action without exposing the issues that separated the ALP and the DLP. We had to be careful in Melbourne in presenting various issues within the YCS. Not so in Sydney where the DLP was weak and there were strong connections between Catholic groups and the ALP. As I Victorian, I was amazed to find that the Diocesan Chaplain of the YCS in Sydney, a Parish Priest, appeared to be the *de facto* chaplain to the local ALP branch.

By the end of the 1960s, Vietnam became the predominant political issue. Differences over conscription, which took effect in 1966, were significant. Many were opposed to sending conscripts to fight but were still supportive of intervention. However, more Australian took the view that the war was unwinnable and/or unjust. When Gough Whitlam announced in his policy speech for the October 1969 that an ALP Government would withdraw Australian troops from Vietnam, differences over the issue within the YCW could not be avoided. Nor could they be contained in the YCS. The implications for the YCW were more serious because it could only work in parishes where the parish priests gave permission for it to operate. The DLP was a strong supporter of military support for South Vietnam. I believe that the YCW's increasing support for the withdrawal of troops was a significant reason for the collapse of the YCW in the 1970s, at least in Melbourne.

1969 was also a year when Senator Frank McManus of the DLP was up for re-election in Victoria. He campaigned on a 'Social Justice' policy, which was a fundamental orientation of the DLP, reflecting its Catholic Action and Catholic Social Justice connections. Although the YCS was established in 1942 as a social justice movement by bishops who issued annual Social Justice Statements, and the enquiries and other activities of the YCS in the 1960s covered social justice issues, the term 'social justice' was not part of the YCS lexicon in the late 1960s.

In reading about eighty pages of the YCS 1968 National Conference Report I could not find even one use of the term social justice. My best guess is that the term was not used because it had become politicised by its association with the DLP. When the term re-emerged in the following decades, often used in conjunction with 'peace', it was seen by many to be a 'left-of-centre' term and rallying point. The YCS's 1992 National Conference Report also avoids the term even though there were many issues covered that we would now regard as social justice issues. Having read some historical documents in recent years, I suspect that the YCS was too late in returning to the term social justice as a description of itself. We still hear of comments from the schools to the effect that they do not need the YCS because they have a social justice group. On Facebook the YCS is described as 'a social justice movement run for, by, and with high school students'. That is a good description, but there is a lot more to the YCS, as we saw in the 1960s.

I now turn to a closer look at the way Vatican II impacted the YCS in the 1960s.

The YCS entered the 1960s with a similar structure to that of the 1940s. When it was inaugurated in 1942 it was anticipated that the YCS would establish and run a wide range of activities within Catholic schools, much like a student council with a wide brief. The YCS therefore ran activity groups such as drama, handcraft, music, debating, literature, missions, and Red Cross. It included some activities that would now be part of the school curriculum. Above this structure was the Leaders' Group which was both formation-oriented and the body responsible for the activity groups. General meetings of all members would be held from time to time.

By the mid-1960s activity groups had fallen away, replaced by groups working through the meetings set out in the widely distributed YCS programmes. Members of the Leaders Group would have responsibility for the other YCS groups.

YCS meetings, like YCW meetings, had three parts: a Gospel enquiry, a personal enquiry, and a social enquiry. The programmes contained Gospel texts with commentaries and questions for discussion. Social enquiries on cultural issues and social needs were in the 'see, judge, act' format with helpful questions, commentaries, and suggestions for using that process. The personal enquiries had two sub-headings: Items of interest and Facts of action. This format was similar to the YCW Leaders' programme. My YCW Leaders' programme from 1966, which I still have, bears out the similarity between the YCS and the YCW at this time, though, of course, the topics for the social enquiries largely reflected the different environments of students and workers.

It is important to stress that this meeting structure had been carefully developed and promoted over the years. This is evident in John N Molony's *Towards an Apostolic Laity*, which was published by the Australian YCW in 1960. At the time John Molony was a Diocesan Chaplain of the YCW. He left the priesthood in 1964 and later became the Manning Clark Professor of Australian History at the Australian National University. The relevant chapter of the book, is at http://history.australiancardijninstitute.org/p/catholic-action-technique.html

The chapter makes the point that the 'Enquiry technique or method' is relevant to each part of the meeting:

> 'Therefore, the Enquiry is the means used by the Y.C.W. which leads the human person to do three things
> 1) To SEE himself in the whole of his life, in his relations with God, with others, with his surroundings in his home, his work and his leisure.
> 2) To JUDGE what he has seen, to judge it with the mind of Christ.
> 3) To take ACTION, either personally or in conjunction with others; action which is formative, educative, of service to others, representative on behalf of those for whom he knows he has responsibility.

The purpose of the process was to transform the worlds (or milieus) in which the participants lived and, in the process, develop a deeper faith. When I first started to become involved in the apostolic side of the YCW it was the term 'formation through action' that was used to describe what the YCW was on about, and limited reference was made to the 'see, judge, act' methodology. The YCW was a Christian formation movement based on action.

The personal enquiry, with its simple headings of items of interest and facts of action, was the critical area for faith formation. In the YCW the priest played a key role. The 1960s was a time when many priests could devote, say, an hour and a half on a Tuesday night for a meeting in the presbytery with the YCW Leaders' group. The resulting personal relationship was very important in the development of Leaders. In schools, there were many Religious Assistants who could provide the same kind of support.

There was, however, a critical difference between the personal enquiries in the YCW and the YCS. In the YCW the personal enquiry discussion often concerned the experiences of the Leaders in their various work situations. By contrast, YCS members met in a closed environment and the discussions of experiences were necessarily limited. More concerning was the possibility that other students might think that the Leaders' discussion of items of interest and facts of action was about monitoring school behaviour and that the Leaders were operating as 'secret police' within the school. A change was made. By the mid-1960s the Personal Enquiry in the YCS had become the Review of the Week and the terms items of interest and facts of action had disappeared. The same kind of concerns lead to the change in the terminology in relation to social enquiries, which were sometimes school focussed: 'see, judge act' was replaced by 'see, reflect, act'. But what was the purpose and scope of the Review of the Week?

When I started with the YCS in 1968 change was already under way regarding the Review of the Week. It came with the Review of Life. That term is now dominant in the descriptions of Jocist movements, and it is generally assumed that the Review of Life was developed by Cardijn a century ago. However, the term was not used in the YCW or the YCS in Australia before the mid-1960s. It is not found in, for example, my YCW Leaders' programme for 1966 or the YCS's National Conference report of the same year.

A sign of things to come was found in the Australian YCW's publication *In This World* of March 1967. It reproduced a paper from the December 1965 YCW International Council in Bangkok on the Enquiry Method, which was promoted as a method for meetings and personal life. It was Cardijn's last International Council. The paper included:

> So, at the base of the Y.C.W. pedagogy, there are three fundamental attitudes which have prompted the "see-judge-act" technique and which express the orientation of the Y.C.W. method. These fundamental attitudes are:
> 1. Spirit of enquiry (to be in search of life).
> 2. Spirit of discovery and welcoming God acting in men and in the world
> 3. Spirit of committing oneself in charity to respond to the call of God.

The document explained the see, judge, act method in some detail and concluded:

> This application of the method is called the "review of life". This is not a discussion of ideas, or an examination of conscience: it is a period of deep reflection based on the reality of life, so as to discover the presence and call of God and to decide together on the personal and collective commitment needed ... This review leads not only to action, but also to prayer in order to return to God all that has been seen and done.

So, the Review of Life was being seen as a way of looking, thinking, doing and praying. It was not only a meeting methodology or technique. In mid-1967 I prepared a programme for the Jocist groups at

Melbourne University which included a two-page explanation of the Review of Life. I still have it. I cannot recall how I got it, but it was almost certainly from Fr Paul Willy (see above) or Fr Kevin Smith, the National Chaplain of the YCW. The Review of Life expressed the YCW spirituality at the time.

The Review of Life approach also came to the YCS in Australia following the conference of the International YCS in Montreal in 1967, to which Australia sent two full-timers from the National Office. The report of the YCS National Conference of May 1968 records the interest in this new development. The main topic of the conference was 'Study', but there were other sessions dealing with a range of matters, including the Review of the Week and the Review of Life.

A paper was prepared by the Melbourne delegation on the Review of Life and a workshop was held on it (see pages 65–70 of Conference Report). The paper commenced:

> There are two foundations upon which Review of Life is based. We believe that God is present and is working and is calling to us through the Human events of our life and secondly, that, when a community comes together the Holy Spirit works among them so that they may discover what God is saying. Review of Life is not a new thing, nor merely a technique, but simply reflection on the basis of the beliefs stated above.

Extracts from the National Report of the YCS National Conference are at the Attachment hereto. You will see from the photo that the conference didn't lack from a shortage of adult participation. The large number of nuns, priests and brothers added a considerable amount of intellectual input.

All of this sat very well with the emergence during Vatican II of the need to read the 'signs of the times'. Basic reading in the YCS in my time was the *Pastoral Constitution on the Church in the Modern World* (*Gaudium et Spes*), which commenced with

> The joys and the hopes, the griefs and the anxieties of the men of this age, especially those who are poor or in any way afflicted, these are the joys and hopes, the griefs and anxieties of the followers of Christ. Indeed, nothing genuinely human fails to raise an echo in their hearts. (No 1)

It was shortly followed by:

> To carry out such a task, the Church has always had the duty of scrutinizing the signs of the times and of interpreting them in the light of the Gospel. Thus, in language intelligible to each generation, she can respond to the perennial questions which men ask about this present life and the life to come, and about the relationship of the one to the other. We must therefore recognize and understand the world in which we live, its explanations, its longings, and its often dramatic characteristics. (No 4)

The YCS senior programme of 1969 had a feature on 'Looking into Life', which drew on, and referred to, the YCW's publication noted above. After stressing the importance of an interest in people and awareness of situations, it explained the purposes of the Enquiry (previously called the Social Enquiry) and the Review. The Enquiry was firmly based on the see, reflect, act process. The Review was introduced by a passage drawing on the 1968 Conference report:

> There are two ideas behind the Review. We believe that
>
> (i) God is present in life, is acting through the events of human life and calls us through these events.
> (ii) The Holy Spirit is working among the members of the group, helping them to discover what God is saying.

The group review was explained:

> The first step in making the review is that each member contributes a fact—an event that has happened, something said, some reaction to an event. The group reflects on each in turn, attempting to discovering the events of life what God is saying and what response ought to be made on our part.

The programme provided a guide to the group review:

> The Review is flexible, but the following is a possible method of procedure:

* What is each one's reaction to the fact? Have we any comment to make?
* What do we think God is saying through this fact?
* Where does this situation fit in with God's plan?
* Is God asking anything of us as a group?
* If we have already acted or made a response in our own particular situation, is any further action possible?
* If we are to make some personal response, what is it to be? Can we strengthen the good we have seen? How can we make our part of the world—where we are—more open to God?

Note that not all of these may apply in every case.

The personal review was described:

> We need the personal review of our day if we are to understand our life, and if our group review is to succeed.
> Thus, we ought to reflect on the events of the day—on the situations that occurred, on the way we responded to them, and the people we met. How was God calling me today?
> There is a close connection between Review and Prayer. The Review trains us to pray about the events of life, teaches us to reflect with God on the real issues of our life. Through it, we begin to integrate our life into the Mass, and we begin to see our need for close contact with Christ through the Sacraments.

These passages were repeated with some small modifications in the 1970 programme. They were very close to the description of the Review of Life I was given in mid-1967.

Perhaps our most frequently quoted book at this time was Michel Quoist's *Prayers of Life*, which illustrated the kind of prayer life the Review of Life worked towards. It contained the following passage in its introduction (which we put on the back cover of the 1970 programme):

> If we knew how to look at life through God's eyes we should see it as innumerable tokens of the love of the Creator seeking the love of his children. The father has put us into the world, not to walk through it with lowered eyes, but to search for Him through things, events, people.

This was the Jocist spirituality of the YCS. It was, in my view, the major change within the YCS in the 1960s.

We can see that here was no reference to the see, reflect, act methodology in the Review, although they are implicitly included within the list of questions. On the other hand, the Enquiry (formerly the Social Enquiry) in both the 1969 and 1970 YCS programmes was explicitly based on the see, reflect, act structure. In both programmes it is stated, consistent with the YCW document of 1965, that the there are two steps in the reflection, the Human and the Christian. In that document the Human reflection is seen as an introduction to the Christian judgment, which is a 'reflection with Christ', with reference to the Gospels. Today we would add references to Catholic social teaching which has expanded greatly since the 1960s.

The 1969 programme recognised the difficulty of fitting the three parts of the YCS meeting into the available time within schools. It was getting harder to find time within the school curriculum or outside class hours. Meetings A and B were on alternate weeks. Meeting A was Review of the Week (20 minutes) and Gospel (15 minutes). Meeting B was Review of the Week (10 minutes) and Enquiry (20 minutes). The same format and times appear in the 1970 senior programme. This was not ideal, to say the least.

This group Review was a big task for a session that is allocated 20 minutes or 10 minutes, depending on whether the meeting was Meeting A or Meeting B. How could it be done in any meaningful way? In practice the Review expanded to fill the available time, to the detriment of the Gospel discussions and the Enquiry.

There were some important questions. Did the focus on the Review of Life present some problems for the movement? Can a mass movement, as the YCS was then, be driven by a focus on the searching questions of the Review of Life? Was the Review of Life a good starting point for student involvement? I should note that my last project with the YCS was to write, along with others, the 1970 programme. I cannot recall how much I thought about these questions at the time of writing, but I did a little later.

A few years ago, I was rummaging through my old YCS documents when I found a handwritten draft of an article that I would have prepared in about 1972, a couple of years after I had left the YCS, but during which I had maintained a close involvement with the Fawkner parish YCS and YCS workers. The article was never completed.

After referring to the move away from activity groups and the adoption of the Review of Life following the 1968 National Conference, I scribbled.

> ... a mistake was made, by myself included, in confusing the aims of the YCS to develop a Review of Life approach, with the method of achieving it. Suddenly groups threw away the old method of Gospel, Personal Enquiry and Social Enquiry and replaced them by a non-directive fluid review. The theory was good-"don't tell them what to do, let them discover it". When starting a group we said "sit down, start talking—we will take it from there". In fact you might be able to take it [reflection and action] from a general conversation, but practically speaking the YCS movement is not able to cope with this at all levels. An experienced Religious Assistant or Chaplain or an exceptional student could make a fist of it, but otherwise negative.
>
> Since then a more realistic approach (the Gospel, Review and Enquiry meeting) has been developed. However, this does still not meet the practical demands of the YCS.
>
> I am suggesting that as a general policy the YCS develop something that harkens back to the activity group era. Basically, YCS groups should be formed for some specific purpose and should be known by that purpose. The purpose should not be a gimmick, but should be [about] a real need in the life of the students and one which the students are able to do something about; and, in doing so, they will achieve a sense of achievement, group spirit, confidence and leadership. In fact YCS groups should not be formed unless there is something which they can do.
>
> The basic thrust of the group must come from the purpose of the group. The group is different from the old activity groups because the group action is not just a label, but something which is worked at, ongoing, reflective, etc. It amounts to a continuing enquiry It is different to groups now doing inquiries because it is more sustained, more satisfying and more work. Having exhausted the action the group might dissolve or, hopefully, seize on something else to do. The first is not a cause for distress.
>
> In a parish or school context, the YCS might have the following groups:

The draft stops at this point. What I was getting at, I am sure, included something like the sustained campaigns on social issues that the YCW undertook in the 1960s. A campaign was an enquiry extended over a number of weeks. In Melbourne the most notable of these was the road safety campaign, in particular the public advocacy and lobbying for compulsory seat belts. However, my suggestion was to run a number of these campaigns at the one time. This was different to the enquiries produced in the YCS programmes where, usually, there was one meeting on each topic and enquiries were unconnected, although in 1969 there were five enquiries around the topic of Study. I was arguing for a social enquiry-driven YCS on social concerns and issues.

I did not seek to minimise the importance of Review of Life. Stapled to the draft is a page headed 'Review of Life', which includes the following jottings: 'R of L is basic to the apostolic formation of lay people'; 'R of L must be seen as an aim and not as a method'; 'We must seek out the most effective methods of developing a R of L approach—problem of methodology'; 'The methodology we use must be of value in itself'; and 'The methodology will be pragmatic, rather than preconceived'.

The point I was making in these drafts was that the YCS should operate with a progression towards a Review of Life approach in meetings and, beyond that, to a member's approach to life generally. The Review of Life, fully understood and not reduced to a methodology for meetings, is the goal, rather than a starting point of the student apostolate, one that seeks to integrate faith and the worlds in which students live.

The following extract is from the current 'NUTS' Introductory Program of the Australian Young Christian Students. ('NUTS' is the acronym for 'Never Underestimate The Students'). It reflects the fact that social issues generally present the usual starting point for the YCS. It sets out a path or journey from social engagement to deep faith formation.

> A major part of the mission of the YCS is to work for a fairer and more just society consistent with the teachings and values of Jesus Christ and the principles and objectives of Catholic Social Teaching.

But the YCS is more than that. There is something closer to home. The YCS also challenges students to focus on the reality of their own lives and the lives of those around them; for example, the needs of other students within their schools and local communities.

But the YCS is even more than that. Engaging with the world, from the local to the global, and working to improve the lives of our nearest neighbours through to those we will never meet will transform the YCS member. Leadership skills, self-confidence and social friendships will grow, not because they are pursued for personal improvement, but because they are the result of a commitment to something above and beyond self-interest.

So the YCS is a 'formation through action' movement. Formation means different things to different people. When we talk of formation in the YCS we talk about Christian formation: where engagement in the world and serving the needs of others is seen as inextricably linked to a commitment to Jesus Christ.

At the heart of the YCS is what is called the Review of Life or the "See, Judge, Act "methodology. It is used by YCS groups as a method or process for discovering, evaluating and acting on a wide range of topics.

But the Review of Life is more than a methodology for dealing with social issues. It is also personal. It is a way of thinking and working our way through a wide range of issues that come into our personal lives, where the judging or evaluating part of the process helps us to better understand ourselves and our relationships with others.

And there is another dimension to the Review of Life that moves us beyond the purely human. The Review of Life is also a process in which our personal and silent reflections on the realities of a commitment to Jesus Christ can become our prayers of life.

The NUTS program will introduce you to the YCS's way of thinking and how it operates. We hope it will take you on a journey of social engagement and spiritual discovery.

In my view, this is consistent with the theology, spirituality and pedagogy that Jocists drew in from Vatican II during the 1960s. The Review of Life in its 1960s form should be understood as a goal in faith formation rather than a starting point. Too often these days the Review of Life and the see, judge, act methodology are secularised, with only a passing nod the Gospels and Catholic social teaching.

In a social justice movement like the YCS, the see, judge, act structure is a useful starting point, but something more is needed if the YCS is to be a formation through action movement. The YCS should not be defined by its starting point or its meeting methodology.

The passage from the AYCS's *NUTS* publication suggests that faith formation is a journey. We could think of the YCS as a train on a journey, a journey that will have frequent stops on the way to the end of the line. Some of those who board at the outset (for example, to only work on a good cause, but no more) might get off at an early stop, appreciative of the good work they have done. But the train must go on; and the job of the YCS is to offer to its passengers inspiration and reasons to stay on the journey.

Despite strength of the theology, spirituality and pedagogy, the fact of the matter is that the YCS and the YCW have lost the institutional support that they once had. By institutional support, I especially mean the support of the bishops. I expect that while the bishops appreciate the social justice work of the movements, their focus in the allocation of scarce resources will be on activities that promote faith formation. Faith formation is intrinsically important, but it is also important because faith formation can also be a means of social engagement and transformation, and leadership development. I believe the funding and other supportive outcomes for the Jocist movements would improve if the Review of Life of the immediate post-Vatican II years were better understood by the movements, bishops and schools.

I had no significant contact with YCS workers and YCS groups between about 1974 and when I was asked in 2018 to join the National Adult Support Team. While I was ignorant of what was happening in the YCS I was very familiar with the content and the application of Catholic social teaching. Leaving aside, as I must, the huge social changes of the last fifty years, which will shape the way in which the YCS now organises, it is important to note the huge expansion in Catholic social teaching and its potential to be a means of changing the worlds in which students live and to deepen their faith.

I am still convinced that the strength of the Jocist movements is in their capacity to achieve three interconnected goals: faith formation, social engagement and transformation, and leadership development. It distinguishes the movements from other youth ministries that are currently better supported than the Jocist movements. If the YCS is to find sufficient student and institutional support, it needs to be a committed social justice movement based on the beliefs, values and principles of the Gospels and Catholic social teaching. I believe this will, be greatly assisted by a closer look at how the YCS responded to Vatican II in the 1960s.

The Review of Life

Extracts from the 1968 National Conference Report of the Australian YCS
Armidale, NSW, May 1968

Workshop 4

Following the National Conference of 1966, the YCS changed the name of the Personal Enquiry, with its "Items of interest" and "Facts of action", to the Review of the Week. At about the same time the

Review of Life approach was emerging internationally in both the YCS and the YCW. In Australia, interest in the Review of Life was prompted, in part, by an article in the National YCW periodical 'In This World'.

WORKSHOP 4: REVIEW OF THE WEEK - IT PURPOSE AND USE

A. PAPER ON THE REVIEW PREPARED BY MELBOURNE DELEGATION

There are two foundations upon which Review of Life is based. We believe that God is present and is working and is calling to us through the Human events of our life and secondly, that, when a community comes together the Holy Spirit works among them so that they may discover what God is saying. Review of Life is not a new thing, nor merely a technique, but simply reflection on the basis of the beliefs stated above.

To know God, we must look to what He is doing in the world. God speaks to us not only through the Scriptures but through the human events of our lives. The Old Testament is the story of secular events, together with reflection of God's People upon these. We must always be looking at what is happening now in our lives for God is calling to us through these events. By scrutinizing the events of our lives and then by reflecting upon them, we can discover the real presence of God in these events. The desire of the dark people in our times for equality and freedom are human desires. God is speaking through their leaders. Some revelation is taking place. God is always revealing Himself if only we can learn to look.

65.

When a community of believers does come together to discover the word of God, there the Holy Spirit is at work. In the Acts of the Apostles, we see that Paul lands at Corinith. On his arrival he joins the profession of tent making with which he was already familiar. God was already at work in Corinth before Paul arrived. So it is that God is already at work in the secualr world today. We should see people, see situations and most importantly see the value that is there.

In the actual working of Review of Life groups each member brings one fact - a reaction to an event. Three or four of these facts will be similar and usually one of these is picked as the point of reflection. The person who gives this fact then tells a bit more about the persons involved, how he felt about it, and the group reflects on the cause and the effect of it. They come then to the question; how is God revealing Himself here through human value interpreted in the light of the scriptures, or, how is God's work being prevented in this situation. Upon this reflection, action is taken on a personal, a group and an apostolate level. Also, if suitable scripture references are found these could be used for suitable prayer and thought before the next meeting. All of this comes in a natural way, in the language of the participants themselves.

This basic method is the same when doing a gospel or social enquiry. We ourselves, must be involved in reviewing our life. Prepare by reflecting every evening on what God is saying to me this day, in all that happened, and in all the people I met. Gos is at work in my present situation.

By doing Review of Life it does not mean that we put less emphasis on the study of scripture or on the importance of doing Social Enquiry. Both of these still have major role in our group. Hence Review of Life provides flexibility which is already present in many groups throughout Australia.

There is a need to be very objective in Review of Life. We have to face the truth. The world and the Gospel are continually challenging each other. We are the point of contact. When one looks clearly at human values we can see through them to Christian values. Since the Resurrection, human achievement has a new meaning. We discover in our reflection human desires, and then step by step we can go deeper by discovering Christian values. We should not be too anxious to impose the Christian aspect of the value that we see, to force insights on others. Allow them to develop quietly.

Review of Life is in fact a deepening of our understanding of Review of the Week and the Social Enquiry.

B. PRE-CONFERENCE PREPARATION

The following questions were asked in the preparation for this workshop by delegations:

1. What value do students see in the Review of the Week?
2. What is brought up and discussed in this section of the meeting?
3. Is it leading students to becoming involved in the whole of life?

4. Do they see any tie-up between the review at the meeting and their own personal review and prayer? If so, to what extent are they reflecting on their life?
5. Are enquiries on the group level developing out of situations brought up and reflected upon in this section?
6. "God has put us into this world not to walk through it with lowered eyes but to search for Him through things, events and people" Discuss.

The following are extracts from the reports received:

"Students' attitudes to the Review varies according to their understanding of it.

Those who find it <u>unsuccessful</u> give the following reasons:

its purpose not clear, the method of conducting it is not clear, the discussion lacks sincerity. The remedies for these are obvious.

Others, and these are now in the majority, claim that the <u>Review is going well</u>, and is leading them to understand the whole of their life better.

It is becoming more common for group enquiries to arise from the situations brought up in this section. Particular mention was made of this by several state high school groups, eg. "loneliness," "teacher-pupil relationships," and the "RI lesson."

<u>Other matters that come up in the Review are</u>:

anti-social behaviour, sport, family and school situations, friends, individual problems."

From <u>Adelaide</u>.

"<u>What value do you see in the Review of the Week</u>?

More than half of those contacted saw great value in the Review. They gave these reasons:

become aware of the needs of others — a chance to know what is going on and to act — make us aware of what is happening around us — people can mention their problems with some view to their being solved. — see the viewpoint of others — makes us aware of things needing improvement, and it brings us out of ourselves, and generally keeps us on the ball.

<u>Their reasons were</u>:

little improvement is noticed throughout the week — resolutions not followed through / individuals — there is not much to discuss from week to week — nothing specific is discussed — we only think of it at the meeting — all talk, NO ACTION! — Some disagreed.

Matters that come up in the Review are:

> Student life - activities at school - attitude to others with whom we come in contact - how to live a fuller and better life - how we can hip in the school - relationships between classes - entertainments - how can we overcome faults - teacher/student situations - our responsibility towards such world problems as hunger and poverty.
>
> One school considered the Review of the Week itself: "We found it was one way to stop kidding ourselves that we were really living as true followers of Christ."

Is the Review leading students to become more involved in life?

> Some said a straightout YES; some said NO. Reason: we avoid becoming personal - only helps in school life - some have found that being really frank with each other has helped make the Review useful in our lives.

Is there any tie-up between the Review at the meeting and their own personal review and prayer?

> Most said YES: about a third said NO."
>
> From Armidale.

Yes - from their own personal review and prayer, they are able to give their ideas at the meeting and then try to do something to improve the situation.

Occasionally bring the problems or situations discussed into their prayers.

Reflection in prayer, although encouraged, is successful at Forms 5 and 6, but one group thinks that there is much to be desired from third and fourth formers. They do not realize that reflection and prayer are needed to complete them as Y.C.S. workers and as people. Second formers still being trained in the idea of the Review.

From Lismore.

Is the Review helping students to become more involved in the whole of life?

> "Yes, because when they examine their conscience, it is with regard to setting a good standard of moral and social behaviour.
>
> Those who carry out their resolution become involved, but, the majority of students seem to forget about it after a few days.
>
> Students admit that from their discussion of problems which concern them, they have come to recognize their own student lives as something to be lived at present - hence they have become more involved in their situation."
>
> From Lismore.

What is the situation?
What recommendations does your workshop make?

68.

C. WORKSHOP REPORT

We feel that the Review of the Week should include the following concepts:-

1. That by looking into the circumstances of our WHOLE life we may become aware of what Christ is doing and how He is calling men to respond in these events. We do this to better hear and respond to the call made to us as students.

2. That Christ is calling to us, through the human events of our life NOW. This is based on the belief that God is a part of our lives; and a Review of the Week is a) a discovery of Christ
   b) a discussion on the reality of our lives
   c) a reflection on these and
   d) action based on this reflection.

3. That the Review of the Week is the students' personal apostolate in which they discover what Christ is asking of them through the persons and situations f their lives. The sharing of these discoveries in a group brings unity and awareness of this apostolate.

To achieve these aims we must be capable of looking into our life situations and to be aware of all that is happening; of attitudes, problems, reactions, community events etc,.

It was pointed out in the National Report that reflection in Australia has been far too shallow. It was found in our groups that we were in agreement with this and there fore we feel that it should be the aim of all groups to endeavour to increase the depths of their reflections.

It was felt that all members must be aware of Christ's presence NOW and His actions here and NOW. If this awareness is present we feel that there is no need to explicitly divide our values into human and Christian values. One point which was made was that we should not ask "How Christ would act in this situation" but rather "How IS He acting. In accordance with this, the area of our interest is the WHOLE world.

The result of the Review, then, is not necessarily seen as an explicit action, but, more a bringing about of an _awareness_; a sharing of awareness, a change in attitude or response. This is action. We do not wish to knock explicit actions but rather we hope to widen the concept of action. Even the fact that you listen and share you awareness with others in an action.

RECOMMENDATIONS.

We recommend that:-

1. Because we feel that the areas of awareness have been limited we feel that the areas of awareness could be in a) our homes, b) schools, c) leisure time and d) world events as reported in mass media.
   It is important that our awareness of these situations should not be too far removed from our own life. We say this because we feel that the WHOLE world is OUR world and therfore worthy of our concern.

69.

2. Therefore we recomend that at least one talk at Summer Schools be devoted to the Review of the Week and within our own Dioceses themselves education in this aspect should be prevalent at training days etc.

3. For the success of the Review, that at night, each member reflects on his day, remembering certain situations and people in which they were involved and came in contact. It is not necessary to be trying to remember every minute of the day.

4. The reflection on facts be flexible. It would be that facts reported at a first meeting be taken from the meeting and one be 8reflected on by each student before next meeting. At the next meeting students share their reflections and actions because this leaves students more free time to make personal reflections on a fact of their own choice.

5. In reflecting on the facts in the meeting, we should try to discover more of the background, the reactions of the individuals involved, causes and possible effects and that we ask ourselves in a spirit of reflection how is Christ carrying on his mission here.

6. That the word ACTION in the context of the Review could be changed to RESPONSE. We recommend this because there seems to be a preoccupation that this section of the Review means going out and immediately doing something. Response would include even a new awareness.

7. That the Religious Assistant and Chaplain participate as members of the group in reviewing their week. We recommend this as we feel that this is essential in promoting unity and trust in the group.

8. That it should be impressed upon all leaders that at the moment at least, Review of the Week should be regarded as an essential campact part of the meeting as should the gospel and social enquiry.

YCS Regional Work, Ballarat and Sandhurst Dioceses; 1971–1972

Trevor Bate

Overview

In 1970, YCS in Australia was expanding with full time workers engaged in all capital city dioceses and some regions to support groups, parishes and schools. The YCS National Executive decided to engage a full-time regional worker in western and northern western Victoria, in the dioceses of Ballarat and Sandhurst (Bendigo). This position was shared between the two dioceses as neither has the sufficient members nor resources to support that a fulltime worker by themselves. However, YCS was changing in the 1970s, along with the Catholic church, schools and society in general. YCS membership numbers were peaking and young people began to move away from the Church. This expansion to engage a regional worker represented the peak of engaging full-time workers. No other regional workers were employed and no replacement worker was appointed to Ballarat or Sandhurst after 1972.

Introduction

My Background

Born into a family with 4 brothers and one sister, I went to primary school at Stella Maris in Seacombe Gardens and St Theresa's at Brighton, and then to Seacombe High School from 1965 to 1969. Our family belonged to the Seacombe Gardens parish and I grew up being involved in altar serving, fetes, missions and other parish activities. During my last two to three years of high school, I became involved in a YCS group in the parish. We met most weeks on a Sunday night.

Most of the members I had known for years through the parish, even though we went to several different high schools (Seacombe, Brighton, Daws Park, as well as Marymount and Sacred Heart Colleges). The meetings included personal review, reflection on gospel readings and review of a few actions, mainly based around social activities and current affairs.

The group was supported by Fr Philip Kennedy, who was the assistant priest to Fr Owen Farrell, the Seacombe Gardens parish priest at that time. (Philip Kennedy became Auxiliary Bishop in Adelaide in 1973 and sadly died in 1983).

In 1968 and 1969, I became involved in the Adelaide YCS executive, with Anthony Regan and Janice Allen who became an Adelaide YCS full-time workers, and with other key leaders. This involvement included attending (and sometimes helping to run) local and national key leader camps, regional meetings and social activities, including the Fifth National Conference in Sydney in 1970.

In mid 1969 I was approached to apply for a position as a full-time worker in Ballarat and Sandhurst dioceses. Philip Kennedy was a great help in thinking about this and supporting my decision to apply.

YCS Regional Work

Situation of YCS in Ballarat and Sandhurst

The structure of the regional position was that I worked for National YCS, based in Ballarat and Sandhurst dioceses from December 1969 to January 1972. At the National YCS level, the full-time workers included Sue Carmen (1969–1971), Liz Whitehouse, Mark Considine (1970–1971), Anne Keogh (1972–1973), Fr Paul Kane (national chaplain 1968–71), and Lorraine Walsh (office administrator). National YCS also supported the Melbourne YCS full-time worker (Margaret Malony) and had a lot of interaction with YCW national and Melbourne full-time workers and chaplains.

This regional work was an experiment to expand YCS into dioceses that could not, by themselves, support a YCS full time worker. Ballarat and Sandhurst did not have the support structures in place to supervise and support a worker by developing action plans, reviewing actions and providing support materials.

In Ballarat and Sandhurst, the YCS organisation was largely based in schools rather than parishes. It was run and controlled by teachers, mostly nuns and brothers. As YCS has a rolling membership where members move on once they leave school, few students set the direction, actions and involvement of YCS.

The following table shows the key personnel and schools in Ballarat and Sandhurst during this time.

	BALLARAT	SANDHURST
Bishops	Bishop Ronald Mulkearns was appointed Coadjutor Bishop in 1968 and took over from Bishop James O'Collins in 1971. I don't remember meeting either bishop.	Bishop Bernard Stewart served from 1950 to 1979. I did not meet Bishop Stewart.[1]
Diocesan Chaplains	I cannot remember their names but there was one chaplain in 1970 and another in 1971.	Fr Gerry Gallagher, at that stage based in Tatura, a small town near Shepparton. Gerry was a great support in planning and reviewing work in the diocese.
Secondary schools visited	St Patrick's College, Ballarat Loreto College, Ballarat St Martin's in the Pines (Sacred Heart College), Sebastopol Marian College, Ararat Mercy College, Camperdown Trinity College, Colac Monivae College, Hamilton[2] St Brigid's College, Horsham St Joseph's College, Mildura MacKillop College, Swan Hill Emmanuel College, Warrnambool	St Joseph's College, Echuca St Augustine's College, Kyabram Sacred Hear College, Yarrawonga FCJ College, Benalla Catholic College, Wodonga Marian College, Myrtleford St Anne's College, Kialla (Shepparton)

---

1. Bishop Stewart had a reputation as a very conservative bishop. For example, his priority was to invest significant funds in the Bendigo cathedral, the only gothic cathedral still under construction in the southern hemisphere at that time.
2. The YCS chaplain for Monivae College was Fr Pat Walsh who went on to become the National YCS Chaplain.

	BALLARAT	**SANDHURST**
		Notre Dame College, Shepparton St Mary of the Angels College, Nathalia Catherine McAuley College, Bendigo (Coolock) St Mary's College, Bendigo (Catherine McAuley College Bendigo) Marist College, Bendigo
Key Leaders	Janet and Pam Canny, Bernadette and Rosemary O'Callaghan, Loreto College, Ballarat Michael Perkins, Paul(?) Howard, St Patricks' College, Ballarat Mary Tehan, St Martins in the Pines, Ballarat Mark Considine, Harry Taylor, Monivae College, Hamilton	Greg Moore Marist College, Bendigo There were others that I cannot remember.

The process for visiting these schools was planned before in consultation with National YCS and the diocesan chaplains;

- Plan visits with National YCS and diocesan chaplain usually around a region within the diocese;
- Prepare content for presentations based on material provided by National YCS;
- Contact school YCS chaplains or assistants to arrange the meeting format and time;
- The format would vary from a presentation to a class followed by discussion during school hours, to attending an after-school meeting in school or parish facilities;
- In some cases, there were separate meetings with interested teachers and assistants, sometimes with the parish priest;
- Arrange accommodation, through the chaplain or assistant where I was usually billeted at one of the students houses;

- Provide summary of activities to National YCS and diocesan chaplain; and
- Provide follow up with students as required.

When in Melbourne, I was billeted with a family in Faulkner, arranged through contacts of Fr Paul Kane.

When in Ballarat, I had an informal boarding arrangement with family there. When in Bendigo, I stayed with Greg Moore's family several times.

Once a region had been visited, I would return to Melbourne to review the outcome with National YCS full-timers and to plan the next regional visit.

The National YCS office provided enormous support, both in planning and reviewing, and personally in coping with the travel and working by myself. When visiting an area, I would be away for one to three weeks, travelling in an unreliable car, managing on a minimal budget and staying in different places every few days. I found the work rewarding but very challenging. I was warmly welcomed by chaplains, teachers and students, and learnt a lot about meeting with different groups of people.

Mark Considine from National YCS in particular, providing invaluable support and mateship, without which I doubt I would have lasted two years.

Social Context

Both Ballarat and Sandhurst dioceses were and still are Catholic strongholds. There was an influx of Irish migrants due to the potato famine in the 1850s, and others to join the gold rush in the 1860s, that increased the proportion of Catholics in the population, supplemented by other nationalities including Italian. The Catholic community developed strong social ties and traditions, especially to counter anti-Catholic sections of society. Religious bigotry was still a part of Australian society in the 1960s.

From the prosperity of the late 1800s, both dioceses were left with a significant infrastructure of churches, including large and magnificent cathedrals, schools, convents and nursing homes.

A large number of towns had a Catholic primary school and the major towns had large secondary schools, including boarding schools for country students. There were also strong social links to many community (football, netball) and professional occupations (police, teachers, bankers).

Politically, the Catholic right, through the ALP (Anti-Communist), the Democratic Labor Party (DLP) and individuals such as BA Santamaria, had strong organisational links to many individuals, parishes, priests and bishops, especially in the Ballarat diocese. The conservative views of the Catholic right influenced the school and parish assistants and chaplains supporting YCS.

This conservative influence on students began to wane in the late 1960s with the trend for more students to take up tertiary education and to shift to the major cities (particularly Melbourne). This corresponded with the changing structures of the rural economy and the decline and closure of facilities in the smaller towns and the decline in rural populations.

Social issues such as the Vietnam war, conscription and social freedoms encouraged students to take more control of their groups and the decisions over their lives. Church issues such as the Church's stance on the contraceptive pill, the role of women in the church and changes to liturgy had an impact on local YCS groups. In the broader community, changes in music and fashion, and the rise of women's liberation and sexual freedoms added to the social and church issues that created a tension between the traditional view of YCS as a faith-oriented group under the control of a teacher, and the more action-oriented view where students were in control and faith-action was more socially oriented.

It should be noted that there were several accusations and resulting convictions of priests and brothers involved in sexual abuse of children at Catholic schools in Ballarat and Sandhurst during the time I was working in this area. If I was wiser and older, I may have picked up indications of this abuse, but I did not and it was never raised with me by any of the students I had contact with. It is chilling to think back about who I met and worked with, and what I might have missed.[3]

---

3. For example, I met with Fr Dan Torpy who was a new assistant priest in Mildura and was the YCS chaplain. Dan Torpy was later accused of lying about the reasons the parish priest, Monsignor Day, was shifted. See: https://www.childabuseroyalcommission.gov.au/sites/default/files/file-list/Case%20Study%2028%20-%20Submission%20-%20Catholic%20Church%20authorities%20in%20Ballarat%20-%20Submissions%20of%20Daniel%20Torpy%20.pdf

There were two additional influences, particularly on the YCS full-time workers: the interaction with the international movement and the influence of academics. Cardinal Cardijn had visited Australia in the late 1950s, and Australian YCS representatives had attended international YCS conferences as early as 1967. Various workers and officials from international YCS visited Australia in the 1960s and 1970s including Johannes Lee and Eric Sotas(?). These contacts brought an image of YCS as much more of a social action movement.

Some of the influential books that were read and debated by the full-time workers were:

1. Paulo Freire, *Pedagogy of the Oppressed*, Herder and Herder, 1970, translator Myra Ramos, originally published in 1968 in Portuguese. This book viewed education as a liberating activity where the student is a co-creator of knowledge.
2. Ivan Illich, *Deschooling Society*, Harrow Books, 1971, a critique of society's institutional approach to education and an endorsement of self-directed learning.
3. Søren Hansen and Jesper Jensen, *The Little Red Schoolbook*, Stage 1, 1970, translator Berit Thornberry, a book encouraging students to question social norms in a format based on Mao Zedong's *The Little Red Book*.
4. Gustavo Gutiérrez, *A Theology of Liberation: History, Politics and Salvation*, Orbis Books, 1971, translators Sister Caridad Inda and John Eaglson, based on the Latin American experience of the 'option for the poor'.

The contacts with International YCS and these books radicalised the YCS full timers and increased the tension between the faith-based and social action-based views of the movement.

Another Task

For the last couple of months of 1971, I was co-opted by National YCS to work with Mark Considine in a review of YCS groups from Sydney to Cairns. We travelled in my unreliable car, using a visitation model similar to what I had been using in Ballarat and Sandhurst where we would meet with the diocesan chaplain and then visit some of the groups. The purpose was to gather information on the groups (size, regularity, reviews, actions, issues) and provide a report to the National Executive.

I am not sure of what happened to the report, but my recollection is that the issues we found reflected those of Ballarat and Sandhurst: groups largely under the control of chaplains and teachers, a rolling membership that meant that groups needed to rebuild every year, focus on personal faith rather than social actions and a tension between a conservative church and students seeking more freedom.

Aftermath

Once I left YCS and started studying at Flinders University in Adelaide, I lost contact with the students I worked with in Ballarat and Sandhurst. Several went on to study in Melbourne and then dispersed into wherever their career took them.

However, the number of YCS groups and members continued to decline in Ballarat and Sandhurst as in all other dioceses. The contributing factors include declining church attendance and participation, declining support from chaplains and assistants, and the other social changes referred to above.

No replacement regional worker was appointed, partly due to finances and partly due to the changing priorities of National YCS. There is no way of knowing if the employment of a regional worker was of benefit to the ongoing structure, content and membership in Ballarat and Sandhurst, and, as far as I know, there is no documented assessment study. While I enjoyed the work and benefited from being in the position, there is no objective view about how this regional work affected others.

YCS in the 1970s

Carmel Brown

---

1. Introduction to the time when you were with the YCS

My YCS experience commenced as a 1965 year-six schooler in a northern Melbourne parish which set up a junior girls' YCS group. My last formal involvement was attending the national executive meeting in December 1973 following a period as the Melbourne YCS 'full-timer' (January 1972 to July 1973). Later, in 1975 I did attend a National YCS conference and in 1979–1980 I was one of two founding staff of the Tertiary YCS–but that is another story! In between and following those years I maintained several friendships with YCS and ex-YCS staff.

Embarrassing to think of now, but as a seventeen-year-old full-timer, one of my first actions in 1972 was to ditch various files of Melbourne YCS groups from previous years. Rewriting history?! Recently, I uncovered a patchy set of notes from that year and located several national YCS programs of the junior and senior YCS days. These were good triggers. The upshot is the following personal and social reading based on the given questions, informed by some documents of the time and a fringe-dweller Church commitment.

I have no accurate knowledge of the numbers of active YCS secondary schools in Melbourne during the junior YCS years. All I can say is that, in 1967, I attended one of two girls' summer training school for leaders and members with forty or so older attendees. I don't think there was a boys' equivalent. In 1972, when I commenced working with the Melbourne YCS, my best recollection is that that there were (minimum) sixteen school YCS groups and twelve parish YCS groups. (For purposes of scale: in 2021, there are sixty-six Melbourne secondary schools and two hundred and ten parishes).

Around that time, the era of larger-scale YCS in schools was coming to an end and parish YCS was being nudged along by more general youth groups. The two Melbourne chaplains brought their YCW experience and parish-based engagement but there was little solid review of ways to work and discernment of strategic priorities. However, the story of the YCS ups and downs is both broader and more nuanced.

2. Situate the time of the movement in church and society

In grade six in 1965, happy to expand home and school horizons and liking prayers and parish, I joined in on the Preston's curate's invitation to participate in a new YCS group. We were two or three groups of Grade six and seven girls and met in a classroom on Saturday then Sunday morning.

Vatican II outcomes were hovering. The setting up of the junior YCS parish group coincided with attention to the role of lay people in Church and world, and the introduction of the Mass in English added to a curiosity if not buzz about what next? Somewhere along the line I learnt that the parish curate set up the junior YCS group to bolster youth connection as we dispersed to various secondary Catholic and public schools. That was less the case with the boys who mainly went to the Marist Brothers across the road from grade five and did not join.[1]

Sitting in circles and being invited to have our say was quite a break-out from religion rote catechism learning, and more generally, silent classrooms. Education during the mid-1960s provided little scope for student input or exploration, and a cone of silence was the order of the primary school day. I cannot recall any regular invitation for student talk outside a regime of question and learned response.[2] Also in my case, on the home front, it was hard to sustain talk due to family size and dynamics. YCS meetings recognised children in a new or novel way. I suspect that that experience was also felt by others.

---

1. I don't recall the chaplain' active presence beyond his instigation of the group. However, in keeping with common chaplains' practice, he may well have worked with our groups' initial leaders–the 14-or 15-year-olds who led us through the nationally produced program.
2. Insightful though it sometimes was, for example, 'why do we have schools?' asked grade four's Sister Ephrem. The rote learned answer included 'to learn to take our part as citizens in the world!

We took our junior YCS meetings seriously and based it on the nationally produced program. The meeting structure and the themes were set. The 1966–1967 junior program for instance outlined the schedule for a leaders' meeting and members' meeting A and B. Key components of members meetings were: (A) personal action/comment on our week, (B) the more social 'enquiry'; (A) the guided reading of a gospel, (B) a chaplain or religious assistant's input. All meeting schedules included opening and closing prayer ('Our Lady Seat of Wisdom . . .'), and for leaders: minutes and general business. The distinction between personal and social was made explicit: each person having a personal apostolate as well as a student social apostolate. The later was most captured in See, Judge Act of the enquiries, the subjects of which included: religion lessons, study, following the fashion, sport.

Action in those junior YCS days was both low-scale practical and focused on internal-developmental or attitudinal change and intersected with mainstream Catholicism; for example, 'is there anything we can do to help other see their responsibilities regarding study—particularly re co-operation with teachers?' (YCS National Office1966–1967). Kindness and care or stepping out were not peculiar to the junior YCS. At that time in our milieu, linking it to gospel *may* have been.

While action was usually individual, being based on the set subject we had something in common. I can recall stepping out to the new neighbour with whom I felt on guard–in this Housing Commission street full of big families. Another action was taking notice of the girl left out in class; and a failed action: how to assist the Italian migrant student next to me who had thirty-two mistakes in eight lines of dictation.

During that time, prompted by curiosity, and enabled by my sister's work stint with the National YCS office, I made my first links with other YCS groups and Melbourne leadership. As a somewhat precocious early secondary student I attended summer schools with forty to fifty older students. Again, the gospel was a strong focus as was the idea of YCS group leadership. This marked the beginnings of my gradual leaning outside the parish group towards a wider YCS world.

The parish group continued in a small form without direct adult backing for three years or so. It dwindled in mid secondary school prior to the instigation of a more general parish youth group (an emerging trend) two years later. In senior Catholic secondary school, I was a low-key participant in the school YCS group, led by a friend, and continued involvement at the Melbourne and national level.

Around 1969 there was a decisive shift in the national YCS focus towards looking more deeply into the world as it was. In schools, there was an expansion of content in religion classes to include much more of life experience (also see section 4). The backdrop was Vietnam war moratoriums and nuclear disarmament marches, the contraceptive pill, the attraction of peace, new music and shared housing; green bans, 1968 Paris student-led demonstrations, Woodstock (1969) and US Kent State University student deaths (1970). Given these currents, the aftermath of Vatican II and the controversy over the Pope's encyclical Humanae Vitae, this was also the beginnings of a drop in church and other institutional authority including schools.

Despite or because of its restrictions and the limitations of curriculum and processes, my own school life had enabled initiative and creativity. For example, I had a school leadership role and with others organised events for year 7s to meet up with other levels; had support for a curriculum change via the religion class; and, significantly, got up to antics with a clever and creative group of friends. Some such initiatives were no doubt assisted by the governing YCS mentality and experience; however, I do not recall any solid review of those actions at school YCS or in the wider leadership structures. In that sense there was a missed opportunity to deepen the notion and experience of movement in terms of society and Church.

It was not surprising that national meetings and publications became more socially oriented and over time less overtly Church connected. For example, the refreshed look national program 'tune in to life' (1969–1970) expanded the sources of 'Judge' to include social commentators; and the examples of the Review included music and the Vietnam war. At that time gospel and reflections were still part of the publication. This stopped with the introduction of bulletins to replace programs. The bulletins highlighted significant issues such as international development campaigns—an example may have been Bangla Desh.[3]

---

3. Archival records not located.

The 1970-on period was also a time of expansion of student voices in the classroom, for example, enquiry-based learning, student participation initiatives, the emergence of community schools, and even school student unions. In keeping with this, 1972 YCS staff read Ivan Illich's *De-schooling Society* (1971) and Paulo Friere's *Pedagogy of the Oppressed* (1968). And to better inform our analysis of political economy, particularly in discussion with an international YCS employee, 1973 staff bought a copy of *Australian Capitalism* (1970)!

I commenced working for the Melbourne YCS diocese in 1972. In Australia it was 'It's Time' year! As a seventeen-year-old, the work was a mixed blessing. The YCS structure and its significant presence in schools and some parishes was weakening, in part due to the social changes already indicated. In addition, and without knowing it at the time, I was missing the creativity with pals, and the certainty and structure of school life. There was less explicit attention to the gospel and programs had been replaced by bulletins.

The outcome of that time was a further weakening of support for the YCS organisational structure and groups but collaboration with a smaller, and perhaps more worldly-wise leadership of students and staff. Applauded actions at this time were anything which assisted the individual or collective student voice or awareness of the marginalised and social structures. I recall a student questioning the fairness of sitting for a scholarship when others needed the rewards more; and the student who organised with others to question compulsory attendance each day of the week. On the job this was mixed with pastoral attention and friendship.

3. The structure of the movements—executive, key leaders etc.

During my junior parish and senior secondary school YCS experience the national YCS structure was clear. Each Australian diocese, set-up an executive made up of students, religious assistants, chaplain, and, where employed, a full-timer. The larger dioceses ran the occasional training days for leaders and members, and summer schools—later called camps. Nationally, there were key leaders summer schools, a national conference (1970 Sydney, 1972 Canberra), and National Executive meetings in May and December each year.

The structure largely remained in tack over time however significant changes in the 1969–1972 period included: dropping key leaders' summer schools and replacing national programs with (if memory is correct) bulletins showcasing campaigns. There was also a period of at least twelve months when there was no national chaplain. When the next part-time chaplain was employed (December 1971), rather than it simply being a bishop's appointment, the national executive interviewed and chose to work with him and with the applicants to the national team. The intention was to bolster the student leadership of the movement. Underpinning this was also a commitment to not impose decisions on others and each other–there were times where this this led to collective prolonged silence!

4. What you saw as the mission of the YCS with the wider mission of the Church

While the junior YCS experience broke a cone of silence for we young students, that is not to say there was no sense of a bigger world at school. Learning to 'take our part as citizens in the world' (footnote 2) echoed a broad Catholic education and social ethos which was still a source of tension in the dwindling Labor Party Catholic schism and The Movement of the 50s and 60s. And, similarly to The Movement, in their heyday, YCS and YCW, especially the latter, were highly efficient and organised recruiters.

Some would have seen the YCS as a source of strengthening youth commitment to the Church and the secular world albeit with less party politics; others perhaps more. My awareness of Church in those early days was heightened during the concluding days of Vatican II (1962–1965). One of its most manifest outcomes was the introduction of English masses which at least enhanced lay visibility if not participation in the Church. Grade five and six students were drilled in the English responses and sat together at Mass, presumably to give it a voice. As YCS little ones we did not dwell on the role of the Church or our role within it, but the group was Catholic and parish-based which at a minimum gave it a footing to a structure which included but was beyond informal friendship. This may be why it survived for several years.

Later secondary school years was a time of some upheaval in the Church: Humanae Vitae (1968); priests and religious leaving their positions; a decline in Church attendance; and in school religion classes gave permission to discuss and ask some questions about the Church and life. Led by teachers, it nonetheless opened the platform for talk by students. This had repercussion for YCS. For instance, the 1969 YCS report in the Santa Maria school magazine indicated that YCS would be confined to senior years as 'it would be better for the first, second and third form girls to take part in class discussions which are not quite along the lines of a YCS meeting but with a common purpose of Christian communication and involvement' (The Marian 1969, 17). Clearly it was a move that reflected the times, not just but including Vatican II.

Chaplains and religious were present at all levels but there was little reflection on role of the YCS in the Church during my time as a student attending national forums (see section 6).

5. Links with other lay movements

My older siblings had been in parish YCW and one had worked with national YCS. So, links with other lay movements was not foreign to me and probably normalised my own YCS student involvement. During my full-timer years I liaised with Melbourne YCW staff. This was on an informal review of life basis. How the world worked (including that of YCS and YCW) was part and parcel of the conversation and the YCW attention to the lives of the less powerful in the world of work resonated with me. There was little student to worker formal contact between the movements.

Between 1971–1975 or so, there was at least one structured meeting which brought together former leaders from YCS and the Tertiary YCS was initiated in 1978 as a companion to the then Tertiary Catholic Federation of Australia. Organisational contact among former lay movement participants has continued via the Cardijn Community Australia.

6. Links with the Church, the good and the bad

Junior YCS, built on the broad Catholic practice of prayer with 'intentions', provided the chance to he heard; supported doing good deeds some of which was be-friending and standing by those left out. At the time it brought Christ to life as distinct from Church rules and catechism. The Summer School impressed on me the idea of Christ as an approach to people (being Christ to each other), not just the source of petition and prayer.

The links with Church during my participation in the National Executive and full-timer working days could be described as one of creative tension. 1971 witnessed the somewhat awkward end of term of the long-standing national YCS chaplain. There was no replacement in 1972. This concretised the shift in direction towards a lay leadership and a more apparent social platform.

The next telling moment for me was some prolonged discussion among the then newly formed 1973 National Team and me about whether to officially attend The Eucharistic Congress Melbourne 1973. The congress was a devotionally based gathering of laity, religious and clerics–still held every three to five years. The decision to not attend turned on whether attendance symbolised support for the hierarchical nature of the Church or did it provide scope for intervention?

The occasional YCS Mass encouraged reflection and commentary. Assisted by that, and the open-mindedness of the 1973 national chaplain, some scepticism regarding the Church gave way to investigation of the YCS relationship to the Church. The question of hierarchy and interpretation were revisited throughout that year: how best to talk with Bishops; would Jesus provide communion to a non-Catholic on the YCS team; where did YCS sit with the Church?

Between us, YCS national staff and myself attended the Australia Bishops Conferences several times. The main contact was the Bishop appointee for youth. It was a small attempt at low-key exchange of perspectives on the state of play re Catholic youth and movement and to a lesser extent the wider world, namely First Nations people.

7. Key individuals you worked with

Across at least eight years of YCS involvement as member, student leader and full-timer, I had formal and informal contact with key local and national staff and students, and two visiting international YCS staff.

Working with key (or leader) students was the order of the day at a national and diocesan level (also see section 3). This didn't exclude YCS staff sitting in on group meetings or giving talks to members, in fact, one of my early work strategies was to attend a group meeting and stay overnight with a leader's family. This was both a strategy of sussing out the state of play in the group and the lives of the members, and a chance for face-to-face follow up time with key leaders.

Given the radicalisation of the movement in the late 60s and early 70s, collaboration with a smaller, student leadership took up a new impetus especially from 1971 (see section 2). In Melbourne, the leadership was the Diocesan Executive comprised of students and a religious assistant. Chaplains were less involved. There was contact with executive members in-between meetings but in hindsight this included support for individuals in personal situations as much as strategic movement building communication.

Identifying leadership and setting a more radical direction was further energised in 1972. For example, a national and a regional staff travelled from Melbourne to beyond Brisbane in a stock-taking trip which sought out students active on education issues. The following year, the national team and I spent some time analysing the state of play across the nation to inform the strategy for development of the movement. The criteria for the decisions were thoroughly examined and re-examined!

8. Where you saw the movement heading in your time both its direction and in terms of it being a social movement of change in society and the Church

In primary school days, the concept of social change did not explicitly register but there was a sense of being part of more caring situations and having a say. As I proceeded with the wider YCS contact, I was more exposed to the language of social change and movement. Enquiries took the form of social study (see) reflection, usually with reference to a gospel (judge) and action on a suggested aspect of life. The aspects included: media, leisure, study, the future.

From perhaps year 10 or 11, I was aware of an added emphasis on social action. This took the form of campaign or enquiry literature published by the national office separate to the annual programs. For example, the preparation for the 1970 national conference included an enquiry on student life. The findings were incorporated in some conference interventions and informed the set of workshop themes to which students expressed interest. The Sydney conference included workshops. (I recall not wanting to choose between interpersonal relationships and social responsibility! I ended up in the former).

Having been used to a structured, somewhat active and creative school life, the 1972–1973 YCS full-timer experience was difficult for me. In hindsight, I missed those elements of school and the daily friendships afforded and yet I was genuinely interested and on point with some of the big picture social and political reckoning of schooling and the world! I did not have the wherewithal or language to identify and express the conflicts experienced at that time. My decision to prematurely leave the YCS work was somewhat impulsive and in part a desire to escape and take up the factory floor work of family and neighbours. I suspect anyone involved in agencies now, would concur that there was a gap in attention to dealing with staff dilemmas.

In hindsight, I warm to the intersection of the early YCS junior days with its simple consideration of the gospel-in-life and the later YCS period of attention to worldly dynamics and possibilities. This was enhanced in1973, when national leaders began to revisit the factors which led to formation of people and of YCS as a movement the Church—not without creative tensions. Those three elements ring true to me for the future of the Church and its mission.

9. If you feel so inclined, feel you have the familiarity knowledge etc to, and most importantly, would like to, please add what you see the YCS experience has done in terms of looking at the future of the Church, its mission, addressing the challenges the Church faces, in this time of heading towards the Plenary Council here in Australia. This is not, however, obligatory and for some will not be a possible or feasible at all to do.

Over the past 24 months I participated in several scripture study series in Melbourne. I signed up on the basis that it resonated, especially in Covid times, and was a fixed time endeavour. Another participant and I were taken aback at *what appeared to be* a by-passing of contemporary social implications of gospels. There was, however, a strong commitment to better understand scripture to deepen personal spirituality and perhaps a strengthened bond to the providing agency.

That experience may not typify the perspective of Catholic individuals and groups in parishes with which I am not in touch. And is there a way of capturing personal spirituality and socially grounded endeavours in the mission of the Church?

I know of initiatives such as Catholic Care, Sacred Heart Mission, Good Shephard services, Eureka St, St Vinnies, religious-led attention to asylum seekers; not to mention Fr Bob in Melbourne, Catholic schools and universities, the annual social justice statement, and media such as the ATF Pressand ABC religion and commentary programs. That is a huge pool of endeavours that intersects with the world. My neighbourhood matters a lot to me, but the above agencies indicate that geographically based parishes and order-based congregations are not the only source of energised Catholic involvement. Some of us will look to specific-purpose enquiries, campaigns, and projects.

YCS in Adelaide from 1974–1975

Catherine Whewell

Introduction

The distinction that the YCS still holds in the world of youth movements in the Catholic Church is its confidence in the capacity of school age young people to have a voice and to act in their own interests and the interests of others for the common good, *within their own educational and social context.*

As I look back over the two years I was the Adelaide YCS fulltime worker, I do so with gratitude for the experience of exercising real leadership in the Church at the tender age of seventeen to nineteen years old.

While the formation provided by belonging to the movement was not profound for everybody, the impact on some who emerged as key and significant leaders has lasted our whole lives. Some do great things, others small acts, but always there is a response because the Jocist method has become the rhythm of our lives.

Writing this brief and potted history of the YCS during the two years in which I was the diocesan fulltime worker has reminded me of the powerful passion for justice that is the hallmark of many young people. It is one of their gifts to the world. The YCS locally, nationally and internationally provided a way of igniting and harnessing that gift, inspiring us to see ourselves as co-creators with God. each with an irreplaceable mission to change the world and build the reign of God here on earth. Quite a mission for school students . . . quite a mission for any of us, even now.

Australian Context of 1974–1975

In the 1970's Australia was in a process of significant cultural, social and political change. In 1972 the first Labor (ALP) government for twenty-three years was voted into national government. The Whitlam era, while short-lived, did make significant changes to Australian political and social policy. There was an energy for change in Australian culture: to be more inclusive of women; to open up the country's immigration program by abolishing the White Australia Policy; to recognise and acknowledge the systemic suffering of Indigenous Australians and their inviolable right to their land; to recognise that Australia already was a multicultural nation by shifting from a policy of assimilation to a policy of integration and diversity. Multiculturalism was regarded as a gift rather than a threat. Legal rights for women were also high on the policy agenda and free higher education with a student allowance that for the first time, enabled anyone access to University.

Theologically, the local Church was making sense of Vatican II. In the Adelaide Archdiocese we had a succession of Bishops who were well versed in Vatican II theology and ecclesiology. Archbishop Matthew Beovich, who attended the Council, was appointed the first bishop to the Australian YCS by the Australian Catholic Bishops Conference.

Archbishop James Gleeson (affectionately known as Jimmy Gleeson) was very supportive. He had a YCS background which gave him understanding of and commitment to the Jocist movements. They were the preferred movements for students and then young workers across the Archdiocese. He visited students on YCS camps, always encouraging us to be people living our faith in the world. He believed in the mission of every person and believed this of young people too. He was passionately committed to the mission of all lay people to be changemakers in the world, realising their baptismal dignity to live the mission of Christ in the social, political, economic issues of our time. As a diocesan worker, I met with Archbishop Gleeson a few times a year. He was a great listener, treated me with respect as a youth leader, encouraged me and challenged me. It was always a privilege to meet with him. His deep faith gave him a humility and graciousness that made an impact on everyone.

YCS During this Period

In the small Josephite secondary school I attended in Aldgate, South Australia, Friday morning YCS meetings were held in place of the religion lesson. The Sisters left us to run the meetings ourselves and were not even in the school building. We had a program to follow. Each week Sister Andrea RSJ, would meet with the leaders to discuss the previous meeting and prepare for the next one. It was a very supportive environment. The YCS provided program topics to do with our lives as young people, however it was more a moral formation program than self-directed analysis and action. However, we did engage with each other about our lives and our ideas and there was a power in that. It was normal for most students to belong to the YCS as I went through high school in the early 70's.

Each year summer camps for YCS group members and formation programs for leaders were conducted by the diocesan worker and chaplain. The Movement was largely Catholic school based, with a few parish based groups. The YCS was the main youth program for the Church. There was a sense of stability as passage through the YCS was part of school life.

Internationally however, the YCS was experiencing a significant shift as young people became involved in life—risking action for change. In Africa and South America in particular many young people were at the forefront of the fight for justice. The 1974 IYCS World Council theme was *Domination*. The 1978 World Council theme was *The Role of Students in the Transformation of Society.*

This sharpened social critique of the YCS as a movement for social and political change made its way to Australia through the visitation to Australia by Johannes Lee,[1] a member of the Asian YCS team. It was further developed with the return of the Australian delegates from the IYCS World Council in 1974.

My understanding of a 'militant' was a student engaged in action against injustice or oppression. Internationally young people were being tortured, disappeared and imprisoned for standing up against injustice. The power of those stories must have brought the RE lesson type YCS discussions here into sharp relief. In light of the International experience, the YCS in Australia was invited to also address the cause and the symptoms of social injustice and act to change them.

---

1. Joannes Lee was an extension worker for Asian YCS. He visited Australia in 1972

Jan Allen (now Bate), the Diocesan fulltime worker for Adelaide in 1972–1973 describes Joannes Lee's influence as strongly focused on shifting energy from supporting base YCS groups to identifying students who were involved in action for change. The YCS needed to become an authentic movement of international solidarity with young people throughout the world, working for justice and against oppression. The South American and African YCS students were risking their lives working against repressive regimes. They became the model of the YCS in action.

The base YCS groups in Adelaide no longer reflected the option of the movement internationally for leaders involved in transformative action in their own milieu. Acting for change provided a sharpened focus and edge to the YCS. There was a new sense of belonging to something larger than ourselves seeking a similar goal—justice for all people.

As a consequence, a major transformation occurred in the Movement in Adelaide.

During this major shift, Jan Allen was the Adelaide fulltime worker, Fr Denis Edwards Diocesan Chaplain, Francis Regan Diocesan President and in 1972 I was a member of the YCS Diocesan Council.

International YCS Team member Eric Sottas[2] from Switzerland also visited Australia in 1973. Jan remembers that he encouraged support of the base movement as well as working with militant students. However, the option was made and resources were redirected to identifying and supporting students involved in action against oppression or for a common good.

Australian participants in the 1974 IYCS Council also brought back an analysis of action for and with the poor using a theology of liberation and praxis model of analysis. I remember attending a conference where YCS Chaplain Mick Burns, spoke about praxis. My own formation in 1974–1975 was provided by national worker Mick Perkins. I hold a vivid memory of sitting by the fire in his parents' house in Ballarat where he led me through Paulo Friere's writing and the methodology of praxis as a way to read the world. I learned about conscientisation; opening our eyes to the real circumstances of our lives; and the call to solidarity with the oppressed that formed the basis of the new direction for the YCS.

---

2. Eric Sottas was a member of the International YCS Team from 1970–1974. He was the first IYCS team member to visit Australia. In 1972 he arrived to work with the national movement, spending time in Adelaide on visitation with Diocesan YCS worker, Jan Bate and the Diocesan YCS Executive, of which I was a member.

National YCS meetings in 1974–1975 were a time of rich discussion about our society, faith and the Church.

During my time attending national leaders' meetings as a student key leader or diocesan worker I met outstanding leaders. Over those years the national YCS Team included Annie Keogh, Mick Perkins, Kevin McDonald, Roger Slee and later Damien Hurley. Pat Walsh was national chaplain.

I have vivid memories of deeply engaging with the gospel through a social justice lens.

We read *Pedagogy of the Oppressed*, Ivan Illich and Gustavo Guttierez. The gospel exploded with meaning and the person of Jesus shifted from someone judging us to someone who was focused on the poor, dispossessed, weakest. We encountered a theology of freedom from all that binds us, with a special commitment and solidarity with the poor. We had a mission to build the world God intended.

A powerful example for me of these 'Judge section' conversations was sitting with Mick Perkins and others leaders in Lowana, the YCS house in Brighton Victoria. Mick asked, in the light of a Gospel of the poor, what could Jesus have meant when he said, if a man asks for your cloak . . . or someone hits you why turn the other cheek? These were not esoteric questions disconnected from our reality. They were engaging, exploratory and transformative.

The level of commitment to understanding who Jesus was and what he was about at the national level of YCS was deeply faith-filled and certainly helped me make better sense of the faith that I proclaimed. It also made the person of Jesus much more real and immediate. While my formation and that of others in leadership across Australia was profound and intensive, the base of the movement in schools and parishes were no longer the main focus of diocesan or national energy or resources.

Of course, there were other social forces that would have diminished the YCS base as other changes also led to a decline in the movement. As religious orders responded to Vatican II, there were fewer Religious available to work with the groups and leaders. Religious Education in Catholic schools was becoming more of an experience of personal growth, rather than personal action or even Gospel focused. RE also needed to be documented and taught systematically, which, while necessary, left less space for exploration. Formation was through education rather than analysis. Actions were more externally focused rather than based on an analysis of the student reality. Perhaps the option for militant students simply hastened the reduction of a movement that was already being displaced? It is also true that the 1950's answers given to us as students about God and the Church and our lives simply were not complex enough to help us navigate our way in a changing world. It wasn't that the theology in the Church was lacking, but the capacity of educators to engage us in our questions, as happened at national YCS meetings, meant many young people simply drifted away and tried to find answers for themselves.

Whatever the complexity of reasons the consequence was the loss of what had been a natural progression for students entering Catholic College, to join a YCS junior group and then move into a senior group.

Instead, a few 'militant' leaders worked to make change in their own schools and communities. While this was a compelling vision of young people changing the world, it also disconnected the base from the leadership of the movement.

During 1973 Denis Edwards travelled to the US to study and Fr Martin White became the YCS chaplain. He was also Catholic Chaplain to Flinders University. Martin saw the need to maintain the normal experience of YCS which he continued in our time working together.

My first memory as the new worker for the Adelaide diocesan YCS in 1974 is ringing every parish and every school to find the YCS. Because of the option for militancy, much of the grass roots movement had withered, apart from a few places where a dedicated adult assistant had maintained interest. It is interesting that when the infrastructure of diocesan worker's visits, regular communication and summer camps ended, the movement slipped away quite quickly.

It was a challenge to try to start all over again. However, there were some new developments with which to work. Two of these, one parish based, the other school based, form the basis of this reflection.

Parish-based YCS Initiative

Fr Rob Egar as parish priest of Morphettvale, in a new initiative for parishes, invited two Sisters of Mercy, Ruth Egar RSM and Meredith Evans RSM, to work with the families, women and young people of a new, large, growing parish in the southern suburbs of Adelaide. These were often families who struggled financially and women who were isolated because they had moved from extended family. There were very few activities for young people. Sr Meredith Evans decided to form a parish YCS group to bring some of the young people from the area together.

The group met in the home of Mary and Pat Steele, an amazing couple with two children, Colin and Helen. Colin, in high school, was a member of the group in my time. Helen became a member later. Mary and Pat really loved the young people who came to YCS meetings and did everything they could to support and nourish them in their often, challenging lives.

As diocesan worker I also attended the meetings. My presence represented the interest and care of the Church, and their belonging to an international movement. In every meeting, we were always part of something bigger.

All the group members went to the local high school. They were not the College educated students that often characterised YCS students in Adelaide.

For these young students belonging to the YCS provided an alternative to their daily lives. Offering a place where they belonged, were taken seriously and were asked to take some responsibility for their lives through action in their own milieu, the school and local neighbourhood. Much of their action was around standing up to be respected.

A drop-in centre was created at the back of the Church to provide somewhere for young people to gather and be safe. They could play table tennis, drink coffee and chat with friends. The YCS members supported this venture and helped take responsibility for its direction.

Being on Church property, the drop-in centre was a sign of the Church's support for the youth in the community. For those who had left school the centre also provided an alternative to the pub, which they couldn't really afford.

These opportunities also provided life-shaping models of how to grow up and shape their lives. When they left school many of them worked in shops or factories. Two were employed by local banks. Some students moved from their YCS group into the local YCW group

Over time, six YCS groups formed in the Morphettvale parish. They participated in leaders' training camps and became part of a bigger movement as the groups in the Archdiocese increased in number with the support of the next full-time workers Andy Sugg and then Kath Kelsey.

Increasingly the YCS moved into parishes so while there were fewer groups in schools, the groups increased in parish life.

A School Based Experiment

When I rang St Aloysius College, a Mercy school for girls, in search of whether they had YCS on campus, the Sister I spoke to, Sr Kath Preece, invited me to meet with small groups of students in Year 10 on a Friday morning as part of the RE program. From these conversations, focused on their school lives, two extraordinary leaders were discovered: Bernie McEvoy and Kath Kelsey.

Bernie and Kath had (have) a strong sense of social justice, they grasped the method and meaning of the YCS and took it to their own situation with intelligence, passion and tenacity, challenging school structures, spear-heading student voices of protest. They were vibrant and dedicated Young Christian Students in the manner that Joseph Cardijn envisioned for young leaders changing the world.

Bernie joined the YCW and became a YCW worker. She remains a dedicated Jocist in her life and work. Kath became a YCS diocesan worker after Andy Sugg, working with Sr Meredith Evans as diocesan chaplain. She also continues to live out of her formation in the YCS in her work as a lawyer.

During my two years working in Todd Building, Victoria Square, the YCW diocesan workers, Michael Campbell and Lesley White, became and remained my life-long friends. Fr Hugh O'Sullivan was the YCW chaplain. Fr Bob Wilkinson was upstairs as Editor of the *Southern Cross* newspaper and next door was the CLM movement with Brian Moylan and Cris Henriksson. I was very lucky to have such a wonderful formative and supportive environment in which to grow.

Towards the end of my time as diocesan worker in 1975, I was given a copy of the documents of Vatican II by Michael Campbell. One of the documents, *The Pastoral Constitution of the Church in the Modern World* has inspired my life and commitment to be in the service of a Church espoused in this document. I was nineteen years old. These were fertile times of belief in a Church engaging with the world that was transformative for both the Church and the world. For the rest of my life, I have tried to live in dialogue with this liberating Gospel.

Bill Huebsch in his books *Vatican II in Plain English* says of Gaudium et Spes:

> *(It) seeks to befriend and engage people of goodwill everywhere to make human life on this planet more dignified, and hence closer to God's plan for us humans"*

Pope Francis encyclical, *Laudato Si'* takes this befriending to the whole of Creation.

The Pastoral Constitution of the Church in the Modern World, is a gift to the Church that has not been fully unwrapped. Some Catholic Social Teaching builds upon this document, but otherwise it remains mostly silent within the life of the Church. Religious Orders' commitment to the poorest and most struggling among us is testimony that they continue to recognise the joy and hope, grief and anxiety of the people as their own. However, in the mainstream experience of Church at diocesan and parish level, this wonderful document has hardly been discovered apart from the opening lines which are quoted on occasion.

> *The joy and hope, grief and anxiety of the people of this age; especially those who are poor or afflicted in any way; is the joy and hope, grief and anxiety of the followers of Christ. Indeed, nothing that is genuinely human fails to find an echo in our hearts.*

The powerful belief about what the Church means for the world, and what the world means for the Church, inspired our YCS and YCW work and has continued to inspire my life ever since.

Why was the formation through the movements so potent for the whole of life?

Central to the formation of leaders in the YCS is the power of recognition and invitation. Fr. Bob Wilkinson saw something in me at a YCS summer camp and as a consequence I was invited to a leaders' camp. Being recognised as someone who could make a contribution, was valued, belonged, viewed as capable of making a difference with a capacity for action, had a powerful effect on my sense of self and my ongoing commitment, as it did for many.

The methodology is praxis based—seeing, judging and acting creates a discipline of reflection: seeking to understand what is happening and its impact on people or the planet; having a framework (faith) to engage that reality so that a judgement can be made about why it matters and what is in need of transforming; being inspired by both to do something to bring about that transformation, so that people's dignity, inherent value and capacity to shape their own lives are honoured.

This cycle of reflection means life is always engaged, teaching us how to live and to love ourselves and each other. Honouring the capacity of each person, together we shape our lives so as to live in justice and peace with all creation. It is a radical invitation to ownership of our lives individually and together for the common good. Our freedom lies with each other.

It is very encouraging to note that the recently published Working Document *(Instrumentum Laboris)* for the Plenary Council opens with the joy and hope quote from the Pastoral Constitution of the Church in the Modern World.

During this preparatory phase of the Plenary Council, studying this document and moving more deeply into its meaning as a whole people, may well help shape the process and outcomes of the Plenary. A Plenary guided by a vision for the Church's engagement with and purpose in the wider world rather than for itself would give us back our heart, as Pope Francis has shown on many occasions.

The *Constitution on Sacred Liturgy* has had a powerful influence on the life of the Church since Vatican II. It is time that the Pastoral Constitution is as well known. Just as they sit together in the documents of Vatican II, may they sit together in dialogue, each enriched by the other.

Our own Bishops can have the final word of this paper. In 1998 the Bishops of Oceania met with Pope John-Paul II. Among their documents prepared for this meeting is a powerful statement about the Good News of Jesus Christ.

> *"Is it true that we concentrate so much on the inner life of the church, the liturgy, the educational structures, the maintenance of essential services in parishes, the struggle to defend the rights and privileges of the Church, that we have become too inward-looking to be able to see the needs of the world around us, to respond to the its spiritual hunger and social injustices? What is the Good News that the Church has to offer?*
>
> *We offer nothing but the Good News of Jesus Christ. Therefore, let us hear what he promised to give to us. Jesus says to us in the Gospels:-*

> *You are loved by God;*
> *Your sins are forgiven;*
> *You are free, even if you are slaves*
> *You are healed in soul and mind*
> *Your burdens will not crush you;*
> *You will have peace in your heart, beyond the peace that the world gives you;*
> *You are called into God's kingdom of peace and love;*
> *You belong to me—no longer an outcast;*
> *You are called to eternal life; and*
> *You are redeemed, set free,*
> *part of me like the branches of a vine,*
> *for all eternity".*
> (Bishops of Oceania 1998 Relatio ante Disceptationem)

And we ask:

> *When have my burdens not crushed me? What helped me to survive?*
> *Whose burdens are overwhelming them? (Incarcerated Indigenous young people?)*
> *When have I been included, felt as though I belonged?*
> *Who needs to be included and no longer an outcast? (Asylum seekers?)*
> *When have I been at peace? How did God help me?*
> *Who needs peace among us? (The whole of the earth?)*

One small step that could make a big difference:

If this statement from our own Bishops was reflected upon as an invitation to wholeness for all humanity and the earth, and brought into dialogue with the Pastoral Constitution of the Church in the Modern World (Bill Huebsch's inclusive version) as part of the study and preparation period or between the Council gatherings, we would finally tell each other about our own joy and hope, grief and anxiety and we would look together to the joy and hope, grief and anxiety of the people of this age (SEE). We would be transformed by telling each other the action of God in our lives and how love, belonging, forgiveness, freedom, healing, peace and redemption are at work around us. We could name the difference it makes to be part of God, like the branches of a vine, now and for all eternity (JUDGE).

And we would know that in return for all we are given we are called to be loving, forgiving, inclusive of the outcast, healers, peace-filled, to each other and especially those who are excluded or suffering in any way (ACT), *to make human and all life on this planet more dignified, and hence closer to God's plan . . .*

Catherine Whewell
With information and insights provided by
Jan and Trevor Bate
Sr Meredith Evans, and
Fr Bob Wilkinson

'Like a Bird on the Wire'
One experience of Australian YCS in the exciting, Tumultuous 1970s

Interview with Pat Walsh, YCS national chaplain 1974–1978

First of all, why the title?

Leonard Cohen fans will immediately recognise the quote. I first heard his mesmerising song in the 1970s when I was working with the YCS. I didn't think I was a bird on the wire then. That image only occurred to me when writing the reflection that follows and I spotted our local magpie perched on the power line across from our house. It was a windy Spring day in Melbourne, very unsettled. The power line shook in the wind, but the magpie, known to me as Calvin after my Collingwood supporter neighbour, maintained his grip. That was me in the 1970s, I thought. Buffeted by strong cultural westerlies and southerlies, I somehow managed to hang on for the ride of my life. To survive and to enjoy it.

It's over forty years since your YCS days, so how did this reflection come about?

Hilary Regan, the publisher of the ATF Press *Cardjin Studies* journal started it! He emailed me in mid-November 2020 to ask if I would like to contribute to a history of the YCS in the 60s, 70s and 80s. Maybe he thought I needed something to keep the neurons fit during COVID lockdown! His pitch was persuasive. 'It may be the only attempt to get a history of the YCS during those times by those who were directly involved', he wrote. He also made it clear that he believed the YCS had something unique to offer the modern church and that the upcoming assemblies of the Plenary Council should be reminded of its potential.

So how did you respond?

I said OK to doing 3,000–4,000 words on the 1970s, on condition I could find records from that time to consult and check my recollections against. I wanted to write, not re-write, history, albeit from a personal and reflective point of view.

I went online looking for a YCS website and Facebook page but couldn't locate a central contact point. A couple of old YCS colleagues couldn't help either. With all the changes of personnel and offices, I began to worry that records from the 70s and previous times had been lost or trashed. Then a glimmer of light. My old friend and colleague Dave Freeman in Hobart, an influential contributor in the late 1970s, said he had some. He was also in touch with a PhD candidate from the Australian Catholic University who was researching how local churches and lay movements received Vatican II, and might have leads. Great project, but he didn't. He was focusing on Hobart.

Then, like the lad from Tangmalangaloo in John O'Brien's delightful bush poem, I was suddenly struck by 'a squall of knowledge'. Maybe those old boxes in our attic were worth a look. And there they were. Driven by caring premonition all those years ago, I had gone to the trouble of boxing and preserving them for posterity but, overtaken with work for international human rights, had forgotten them.

The boxes contained some 300 files. Pure gold waiting to be mined. They include YCS publications from the 40s to the 80s, programs, national and international conference reports, notebooks, exchanges with dioceses and international YCS, address lists, correspondence with the Bishops' conference and so on. Even a YCS minute book from 1947. In it, recorded in handwriting, are the proceedings of meetings that involved people like Bob Santamaria and notes on visits to the first schools in Melbourne to take on the YCS.

I was simultaneously embarrassed and relieved. Also, to be honest, I was a bit annoyed to find that a nice publication commemorating fifty years of the YCS made no mention of me or of staff like Roger Slee, Anne Keogh, Trevor Bate and Kevin McDonald who'd put their careers on hold to work for the YCS. Having the archives also meant I had no excuse now not to write for Hilary Regan's publication. I submitted a general overview. But I very much hope that a professional PhD student or historian will write a proper history. Also that the archives find a good home and are digitised and made accessible for research. What follows are little more than rough notes so that at least one experience of the exciting and tumultuous 1970s is there to consult, for what it's worth.

How did you first become involved with the YCS?

I was not in the YCS at school. I only became involved as a young adult priest and teacher in the late 1960s. I wonder now would I have taken on a chaplain's role had I been in YCS at school? Would an early experience of the YCS have formed me in what St Therese of Lisieux called 'un bruyere d'amour', a commitment that burned deep enough to inform the rest of my life in some way, or would it have been water off a duck's back? I'd like to think the former. I agree with an observation Christine Perkins from those days made to me recently. 'As a young person,' she said, 'YCS taught me to look beyond myself. It gave me a vision which has expanded over time and shaped my whole life.'

My first experience of Jocism was attending a Young Christian Worker (YCW) summer school for seminarians at Lowanna in Melbourne. It had a decisive impact on me. The impressive presenters (young lay leaders and the charismatic Fr KJ Smith) and Joseph Cardijn's work gelled with my reading about the exciting priest-worker movement and other social apostolates for the marginalised in France. It also fitted well with new emphases coming from the Second Vatican Council on the lay apostolate, the unity of faith and life, and engagement with the world. Aged twenty-four and newly ordained, I came away committed to making the principles of Jocism integral to my future work, whatever that might be. I also came away with a YCW perspective, not one informed by the Melbourne YCS model of the day.

What impressed you about Cardijn?

It was a case of the medium being the message. I never met him so my impression was second hand and mediated by those YCW people I met at Lowanna. Like a religious order or civil society organisation that epitomises and projects the founder's charism, these YCW had caught the Cardijn bug and given it to me.

In essence, what struck me was Cardijn's belief in ordinary young people, and his concept of priesthood. Both amounted to a direct challenge to the church model of the times which was too aligned to the establishment and too clerical. As a child of working class parents in Belgium who, following his enrolment in the church, was scorned by young workers for joining the elite, two things became self-evident to Cardijn. One, that the church and priests were badly amiss to ignore youth who worked in factories from which, as Pius

XI famously said in 1931, 'dead matter goes out improved whereas men are corrupted and degraded'. And two, that working class youth themselves, loved, believed in, organised and trained, could be 'subjects' of their own development and evangelisation. For this he developed his famous see, judge, act method of formation. Vatican II saw that the method had wider application and endorsed it including for schools. It also influenced the development of Paulo Freire's famous pedagogy of the oppressed, as it did liberation theology in poverty stricken Latin America.

Cardijn's first love was working youth and the YCW; I don't know what he thought of the YCS. I doubt he disowned it like an illegitimate child but I wouldn't be surprised if he was ambivalent. Years later, visiting Hong Kong in 1967, he lamented that not one priest had been released to work with working youth there while thousands of priests all over the world were occupied with the education of middle class youth. I imagine he thought that, at the very least, Catholic schools should ensure that their 'products' went out into the world and the church with 'improved' social consciences and a strong sense of their unique vocation as lay people.

Though not new, Cardijn's recognition of the potential of youth as a force for change was spot on. It remains so. The impact motivated students can have is clear to any observer of contemporary affairs. Greta Thunberg, the students of Hong Kong, and the 90s generation in Indonesia who overthrew Suharto and created the conditions to free East Timor, all ask the church, as Cardijn did vis-à-vis working youth: where are you in all this?

So how did you put your Lowanna experience to work?

Ironically, my first job after ordination turned out to be teaching at Monivae College in Hamilton, Victoria. A provincial centre of some 10,000 people, Hamilton was not at first sight the most obvious place to put my enthusiasm into practice! But the college and the town soon presented openings.

Academically, I was able to introduce a third world language, Indonesian, to the curriculum and open young minds in a country of 'the centre' to a country on 'the periphery', to use later International YCS (IYCS) language. As a teacher of religion, I asked senior students to value their future role as lay Christians, and not feel lesser Catholics because they didn't 'have a vocation' to the priesthood.

My apprenticeship deepened when I engaged with life outside the college. I learned that 'day students' felt alienated in the majority boarding school and suffered small town blues. Though within Malcolm Fraser's electorate and boasting it was the wool capital of the world, Hamilton struggled with economic depression, youth unemployment, lack of opportunity, exodus to the city and associated loss of confidence and civic pride. The situation peaked tragically in 1971 when two local eighteen year old boys sadistically murdered a local fifteen year old school girl, generating unwanted publicity and further anguish in the town.

In response, I introduced the YCS to both boarders and day students. Sharing membership in the same organisation may have helped level the playing field, but was probably more helpful to the day students. As a form of 'official' outreach on behalf of the college it made them feel the college cared a bit more. It was a space that was their own, in which they could share freely and seriously with trusted friends, including about faith, take responsibility for an organisation, socialise and have fun. The YCS also engaged with the town in other respects. It came to include girls and students from non-Catholic high schools. To considerable acclaim, it established and managed a drop-in coffee shop for local youth, got good support from the local council, parents, the local member of State Parliament (Bruce Chamberlain), the press, and several aspiring entrepreneurs. YCS also did its bit to support Action for World Development (AWD) and local groups involved in Third World development, produced a newsletter, and participated in the Ballarat diocesan YCS.

My scrappy diary at the time reminds me that Bob Santamaria and his National Civil Council (NCC) were active in the area and that I attended several of their briefings. This is not surprising given that Malcolm Fraser and Santamaria shared similar world views and were in contact. The NCC's concern was not schools so much as hotbed universities that naïve school leavers were heading to. Universities like Monash were depicted as ideological battlegrounds on which the future of Australian society was being decided, for better or for worse, as graduates came to occupy influential positions in commerce, education, media and politics. Invoking the famous dictum attributed (perhaps wrongly) to Edmund Burke that 'The only thing necessary for the triumph of evil is for good men to do nothing', Paul D'Astoli warned that a minority of Trotskyist, Maoist and SDS (Students for a

Democratic Society) revolutionaries were free to 'terrorise' Monash because most students just focussed on getting a degree and having a good time.

Other than in books, this was my first exposure to political analysis of this kind. As will become clear, this perspective was consistent with the orientation of the YCS of the 40s and 50s but went further by calling for a direct engagement with the enemy. As will also become clear, YCS in the 70s identified a different enemy, viz global capitalism. as the principal challenge, but, ironically, also grounded its critique in social Catholicism.

For its part, the YCW resisted pressure to be used by the NCC. Like Cardijn when he refused to make the YCW a trade union, or protected the independence of the YCW by getting papal support to prevent its absorption into a general youth movement, Fr Lombard, the YCW chaplain, insisted that young workers had to grow in their own analysis and orientation. Though a key supporter of Santamaria, Archbishop Mannix reportedly told Lombard to proceed as he thought fit.

A number of YCS students, all day students, from that time have been lifelong friends. In addition to me, some like Mark Considine, Damian Hurley and Roger Slee went on to work fulltime for national YCS, Roger probably the only non-Catholic to do so (in 1973).

What was happening in Ballarat at the time?

The diocese had an active YCS program, including summer schools, and more broadly, championed the lay apostolate. Backed by Bishop James O'Collins, who had confirmed me, it hosted an Adult Lay Apostolate centre at 42 Sturt Street that provided a range of services, including support for the YCS and YCW. In 1967, galvanised by the 'spirit of initiative and responsibility . . . that has quickened and intensified remarkably in the wake of the Vatican Council', the diocese held the first lay convention of its kind in Australia. The convention discussed how key Vatican II documents such as the *Decree on the Laity* could be implemented in 'the real life situations of our people, in our diocese, in our times' and tackled world poverty and peace. Contributions were made by respected lay leaders such as Gerald Caine, Jim Ross, Garry Eastman, Pat Goggin, Elizabeth Ross, and Frank Sheehan. It also served to prepare delegates to the forthcoming World Congress of Laity in Rome whose Australian delegation was led by Bill Byrne.

Looking back from 2021, what did you learn from your experience in Hamilton and Ballarat?

My work contributed in a small way, possibly more by osmosis than anything, to the development of student leaders across the diocese. Besides those already mentioned who went on to work for the YCS, others like Judy Kennedy, Bernadette Prunty, Genevieve Timmons, Rosie Callahan and Christine Perkins, went on to give exemplary service to society at home and abroad. Michael Perkins, a St Patrick's College old boy like me, also worked nationally with me for two years. Mick tragically drowned in East Gippsland in 1976 while on a camping trip with our YCS colleagues Kevin McDonald and Lorna Payne, due to his epilepsy we think.

I can think of three key lessons from those seven years. First, I prioritised action over reflection, divorcing rather than marrying them to add value to both. I made problem-solving action the end point, undervaluing the potential of situations for further inductive formation via reflection and analysis, including faith inquiry and prayer. Trevor Bates (who worked for the YCS in Sandhurst and Ballarat at the time) and Kevin McDonald challenged me to do this, but in vain. Second, I neglected the student character of the YCS. As a teacher, I was in a unique position to encourage deeper reflection by the YCS on college life and education. Colleagues from other parts of the diocese such as Frs Bill O'Connell, Paul Mercovich and Noel Torpey were not so well placed. For them as curates, the YCS was more a parish activity and youth group. And lastly, the YCS did not continue for long after I moved on. I had excellent support from people like Sister Maureen Keating, John O'Loughlin and others but I had not effectively mentored a successor at Monivae.

How did you become YCS national chaplain

The short answer is Mark Considine. Mark moved from Hamilton to work for national YCS 1971–1972. Anne Keogh, Carmel Brown (Melbourne YCS) and Trevor Bate (regional YCS) also worked in the national office, then upstairs at the front of Central Hall at 20 Brunswick St, Fitzroy. A former boot factory, the hall had been turned into a Catholic meeting venue by the Melbourne archdiocese. It later became the renowned TF Much Ballroom where bands like *Daddy Cool* and *Midnight Oil* played; it is now part of Australian Catholic

Bill Armstrong, probably not long after he'd returned from working for the International YCW in Brussels, he challenged me to think how I would live my priesthood. Later we were to collaborate in the defence of international human rights for many years.

In Australia, the *aggiornamento* of the YCS was led by impressive lay leaders like Suzanne Carmen, Brian Lawrence, Elizabeth Proust and Anthony Regan. In 1972, it was built on by Mark Considine and Anne Keogh, then continued in 1973 by Michael Perkins, Roger Slee, Kevin McDonald and Anne Keogh. They emphasised engaging with the big issues of the day such as apartheid and political imprisonment in Vietnam and Indonesia, and looked to people like Fr Bob Wilkinson and YCW leaders like Tim Walsh, Frs Frank Hornby and Michael Casey for ideas. When she visited Sydney for national YCS, Anne Keogh billeted with YCW in Redfern who were active on Aboriginal concerns. Later, this sense of common cause with YCW contributed to collaboration and socialising with YCW staff like Mark McPherson, Mick Campbell, Kath McPherson, John Bonnice and Terry Daniels.

International YCS also became more significant in Australia during this period, adding to the momentum for change. In 1971, Anthony Regan and Suzanne Carmen attended a YCS meeting in Singapore. Johannes Lee (IYCS extension worker based in Singapore) and Eric Sottas (a Swiss staff member at the international secretariat in France) visited Australia in 1972 and 1973 respectively. They formed strong bonds with national YCS and Mark Considine in particular. Student action to deepen faith, analysis and commitment was the centrepiece of their message to Australian YCS.

This search for a more authentically Cardijnian, lay-led and student focused YCS was to characterise the YCS throughout the 1970s. It also generated a fraction too much friction, including in and for me!

Can you say a bit about the big moments of your first year as national chaplain

Like a weather map, 1974 was a year of highs and lows.

The YCS national executive asked me to work first in Melbourne. As I was new to Melbourne and the job, this seemed like a good idea.

However, YCS in Melbourne, or least its chaplains, politely resisted my advances! Frs Ernie Smith and Mick Morgan, both energetic assistant parish priests, preferred parish to school-based or focused YCS.

The national YCS approach, they said, was 'difficult to fully understand' and 'non-productive'. Citing what divorce lawyers call 'irreconcilable differences', I told the executive I had to back off. Rather patronisingly, I blamed the chaplains for the problem. I reported they treated students 'as the objects of their vertical apostolic activity'! The chaplains and I, however, stayed in touch and later they attended several national workshops for chaplains and assistants.

Refusing to be beaten, I switched my attention to schools in the less privileged inner and western suburbs where YCS seemed more relevant but didn't exist. I also checked out housing commission flats and youth centres and considered living at the All Saints parish at the southern, depressed end of Fitzroy. Though well intentioned, none of this worked out. Establishing a new organisation required long-term immersion that by definition was not possible for a blow-in with national responsibilities.

Not being welcomed in Melbourne, the heartland of YCS where it first started and after all the excellent work of people like Carmel Brown, was a setback. In September, I was delivered a similar message in Sydney. Bishop Edward Kelly, an MSC like me and my former superior, told me that national YCS was not welcome in Sydney. He denied 'rumours' that national YCS had been banned but said it 'had done enough in Sydney for the time being' and that contact should be limited to Fr Ron McFarlane and myself. 'Melbourne people', he said, had made a bad impression, had sown division and, according to a report from a NSW state conference, 'were humanitarian and had no place for Christ'. Some other bishops, he concluded, were likely to follow Sydney and run YCS independently in their dioceses.

The stand-off by Sydney did not last. Amongst other things, the archives tell that Sydney YCS contributed to the 1977 edition of *Student Bulletin*, was well represented at the 1978 national conference held at my old school in Hamilton, Victoria, and elected to the YCS national executive.

Tasmania, thankfully, gave me a much warmer reception than the big mainland dioceses. Later in 1974, I worked there for some three months. Tasmania had a strong Jocist tradition, perpetuated by the likes of Frs Graeme Howard, Terry Yard, and Julian Punch. My itinerary included YCS groups in Devonport, Longford, Ulverstone, Launceston, Georgetown, Hobart, Dunalley, and Cygnet. Unlike Melbourne and Sydney, these were more than youth groups. They reviewed real situations and engaged in school related action as best they could. They also benefitted from the presence and leadership of young laity like Paula Daly, Mary Harrington, Mercia Bresnehan, David Freeman and Rosie Huxtable. Key adult supporters like Fr Mick Byrne, and Sisters Liz Compton, and Prue Francis became valued friends. Liz Compton and Dave Freeman, a student at St Virgil's when I visited, went on to give important and creative service to national YCS.

The balance of 1974 yielded three significant and more positive experiences.

In April, with colleagues Kevin McDonald and Michael Perkins, I attended a three day workshop with Paulo Freire in Belgrave in Melbourne. At the time, the bearded, Brazilian, Catholic educator enjoyed guru status and his critical pedagogy owed much to Cardijn's method of formation. Mark Considine had given me Freire's *Pedagogy of the Oppressed* (1970). Mick Perkins (visiting Maitland YCS at the time) captured the star power Freire enjoyed amongst us when he wrote in pencil on the outside of an envelope bearing a letter to the national office: 'Make sure you let me know when Paulo Freire is coming to Melbourne!' He didn't want to miss out.

Education, Freire told us, is never neutral. It either serves those in power or it serves liberation. He advocated learning from experience, not only books or teachers, a lesson it took me many years to appreciate, raised as I had been to defer to external sources. His radicalism, he said, was 'the result of my Christian belief and formation, helped by Marx with whom I have no problems, but I am not a Christian, I am becoming a Christian.' The question is, he said: 'What is the task of Christians at this point of history? What sort of society do we want to create?'.

Freire's critique was amplified in another hot title, Ivan Illich's *Deschooling Society* (1971). Illich, another Catholic thinker writing from a southern and Cardijnian perspective, also advocated critical pedagogy that drew on learning from and analysing experience. 'The most important thing you learn at school', he said, 'is that learning only happens by being taught'.

One couldn't have wished for a better preparation for the World Council of the IYCS that followed in July-August in the Netherlands. I attended with Kevin McDonald, Mark Considine, Fr Geoff Aldous (Perth), and Fr Wally Dethlefs (Brisbane).

Though not to be missed, the Council was not for the faint-hearted. Over twenty-nine intense days, participants from forty-one countries analysed the world (with the help of Professor Nicos, an economist from the University of Paris) and reflected on what it meant for the IYCS from the perspective of liberation theology (assisted by Fr Gustavo Gutierrez, author of the highly influential book *A Theology of Liberation*, and chaplain to the YCS in Peru). The Council was a triumph for the dynamic Latin Americans. Raquel Rodriguez (Uruguay) was elected secretary-general and joined by two other YCS from 'the periphery', Agnes Joseph (India) and Mwanitu Kagubilla (Tanzania). The YCS was re-oriented to engage in transforming a world order judged to be unjust and exploitative (that is, dominated by 'the centre' or rich countries over 'the periphery', the poorer societies of Latin America, Asia and Africa) and at odds with the theology of the Incarnation and love of neighbour. The Council allowed that the development process of secondary students (absent, incidentally), had to be respected, but students generally were challenged to think big, to see themselves and education as a force for critical change, liberation and evangelisation, rather than simply a prudent career choice. We were also encouraged to collaborate with like-minded siblings such as YCW and the International Movement of Catholic Students (IMCS).

Some of us recovered by heading to Switzerland. As guests of the lovely YCS chaplain Jean-Pierre Catry, we picnicked on wine and cheese on a green slope in the majestic Alps. Then, no doubt wanting to pay our respects to the pontiff, we took the train to Italy hardly daring to look out the window down the precipitous drops. In Rome we crashed at the MSC head house at Via Asmara for a few days, photographed ourselves as Roman senators robed in sheets from our beds, dined on pasta, and marvelled at Michelangelo's Pieta (sadly through glass, after its 1972 vandalisation), before heading home to reality.

The World Council reminded us that we were close to Asia and, as an established YCS of the 'centre', could take up the IYCS cause by connecting to students in Asian countries. En route to the Netherlands in July, Kevin McDonald and I visited Indonesia only to find the lay apostolate there primarily preoccupied with communism. A year later, some of these laity were to advise General Suharto on the takeover of East Timor. At the Council, we also met with delegates from New Zealand, India, the Philippines, and Singapore to explore regional cooperation and mutual assistance. In 1976, this led to our participation in a regional conference of Asian YCS in Thailand. In 1977, Fr Mick Byrne from Tasmania visited the Pacific and attended a regional YCW gathering in Fiji on behalf of Australian YCS. The 1978 edition of our YCS directory included contacts we had in PNG, New Zealand, the Pacific Islands, Indonesia, Singapore, India, The Philippines, Hong Kong, Thailand, Malaysia, Pakistan and Sri Lanka. In 1999, I and a group of students explored the prospects for YCS in East Timor. Today, YCS has members in seventeen countries in Asia, supported by a regional secretariat in Manila.

Lastly, sometime in 1974, I moved into a rented share house with Mark Considine and friends at 528 Brunswick St, Fitzroy. '528' has a special place in the YCS story. Situated across the street from YCW house, it became the unofficial HQ for YCS, a welcome house to others including interstate visitors, and then the national office of the YCS in 1976 when Lorna Payne and I were the national YCS team. I had canvassed the idea of non-institutional living in Hamilton and with MSC colleagues in Canberra, the idea being to live and bear witness in the community not apart from it. At '528' we made valiant attempts to live as Jocists. In the spirit of the times, we tried living simply, dressing down, shopping in bulk, running chooks, sharing housekeeping and bills, reviewing our lives and faith and celebrating the Eucharist around our kitchen table. Let's just say, it was a creative project worth examining further at some stage for do's and don'ts. Fr Mick Bryne undertook a similar venture with YCW leaders in Hobart.

What were the main issues of the rest of your time?

The archives remind me that I attended a mind-boggling number of meetings over five years, particularly up and down the east coast. Many of these involved minute, even painstaking, examination of a plethora of local and individual experiences.

This approach was consistent with the method advocated by Cardijn, Freire and Illich. It was to work inductively, from experience, not to teach top-down in the traditional way. In hindsight, however, I think we risked losing sight of the wood for the trees . . . drowning not waving!

As national staff, maybe it would have been more helpful, and less demoralising, to have left the nitty gritty to locals and given more attention to method, principles, vision and their theological rationale. Framing study as a vocation and pathway to building the just society in Australia and the world envisaged by Vatican II might have helped students lift their heads above the tedious, daily round of classes, essays, and exams and made more sense of school. It would also have required an enhanced level of theological literacy and spirituality on our part.

With the benefit of hindsight, I can see now that there were at least four burning issues at the time: the review of life; the student character of the YCS; its lay character and the related issue of chaplains and adult assistants; and the mission of secondary school YCS.

What was national YCS' concept of the Review of Life?

I will tackle this together with the second issue mentioned above. For us, the review and student character of the YCS were two sides of the one coin.

Life is a big word. It automatically evokes existence itself, meaning, purpose and big questions like 'why are we here' and 'what is it all about'? Even for a teenager, perhaps particularly for a teenager, it also covers a broad spectrum of everyday involvements and concerns: home, family, relationships, music, social media, substance abuse, school, faith, future, dress, health, hobbies, and the journey towards self-confidence and maturity, each a multi-dimensional composite.

So what did YCS mean by life? In the 1970s, we meant life at school, the equivalent of the workplace or factory to the YCW. YCS were encouraged to focus on school analytically, both as an experience and as an institution. To us, the 'see' part of Cardijn's method meant drilling down to deeper levels. We wanted the school itself, not just the curriculum, to be studied. Schools are key institutions in society, State-mandated and resourced to serve the interests of society and economy. They are a window into macro-society, its priorities, direction, and values and, to a certain extent, a microcosm of the world students are being equipped, or as some see it, engineered, to join. No matter how seemingly insignificant at first glance, incidents or experiences at school reviewed in-depth could show how school and society worked, their power structures, practices and relationships. 'Judged' against Christian ideals (step two of Cardijn's method), these uncovered facts might reveal counter-values to the Gospel and invoke calls to 'act' (step three). Repeated, this cycle of action and reflection would deepen understanding, faith and commitment. Fr Ben Pelegri, a Spaniard appointed international chaplain by the Vatican following the 1974 World Conference, sharpened this concept during his visits. He formed a close working bond with Fr Bob Wilkinson, reframed the review of life in terms of values and counter-values and encouraged YCS extension into the tertiary sector. This would take YCS to a new, unexplored level in Australia and provide a future pathway for committed secondary YCS alumni. With Bob Wilkinson, several ex-YCS pioneered this Tertiary (TYCS) initiative, including Francis Regan, Sharon Oates, Carmel Brown and Kevin McDonald. Later, TYCS collaborated as sibling organisations with the Tertiary Catholic Federation of Australia (TCFA) and their national staff, Linda Wirth, Peter Ryan and Colleen Foley.

In 1975, at the YCS national conference organised by Damian Hurley and myself at Monash University, I used the following example to illustrate how the review of life could be an instrument of conscientisation and faith building. Toilets at a school in Gilgandra had been defaced with offensive graffiti. Responses by the staff, YCS and SRC varied from disgust, to removal, to disciplinary action. At one level, this process was an example of an effective YCS review and action. Further reflection with the YCS, however, exposed a bigger issue, one that called for a different and deeper response. Aboriginal kids were responsible for the obscenities. This in turn led to an enquiry into the source of their alienation, a new level of awareness, understanding of faith, and action. The example also illustrated that engagement with people, not just workshops (as Freire had reminded us in 1974), was critical to learning.

Was this focus on school too narrow, even Bolshie? As indicated, some dioceses believed it was. They felt that it ignored the wide range of teenage needs; favoured a YCS elite over the general membership, and encouraged militancy. Some were outraged at the suggestion that Catholic schools were oppressiive. Others, on the other hand, believed the only way to conscientise youth in an 'option for the poor' was to forget schools and engage YCS with disadvantaged kids outside the school setting.

The approach also rebounded on national staff. We were accused, sometimes correctly, of having an agenda, of favouring students who'd engaged in 'authentic student action' and prioritising analysis of situations over the faith dimension. Working in places where a different YCS model was entrenched became awkward and challenging. On the other hand, Brisbane YCS questioned our credentials, arguing that our lack of local involvement and the very notion of itinerant, fulltime national staff was a contradiction in terms. All fulltime staff, they believed, should have a local engagement and function from that base. This partly explains why there were only two national staff in 1975. It also led to longer stays in several dioceses.

In self-defence we referenced the challenge about identity that Cardijn had given the YCW years before: 'A dramatic society, table tennis team, youth club of young workers for the sake of young workers, is not the YCW. Emphatically not. Get deep into this problem, it is absolutely fundamental.' The YCS, we responded, is what its name says it is. A movement of formation in awareness, Gospel values and responsibility for and about students as students.

Around the same time, YCW was asking itself similar questions. In response, several YCW chaplains and staff went to work in industry to re-connect with the work experience and refresh their understanding and authenticity. In 1978, Barry Dwyer, a Sydney lecturer in education, boosted our confidence in our approach. Addressing the YCS national conference, he reminded us that schooling owes a lot to the industrial revolution, and to military and factory practices. Drawing on relevant Vatican and other official church statements, he presented an inspiring alternative vision of what a Catholic school could become. We reproduced his talk in the national YCS *Student Bulletin* (issue 5, August 1978).

Granting that student life should be front and centre of the review, should review also make room for other life experiences and challenges? I believe so. Students are not disembodied minds or part-time humans. The whole person needs nurturing in a balanced way. This also means fostering a YCS that embraces play and socialising.

How did you promote the lay character of the YCS without losing adult assistants?

The obvious tension between the two was captured neatly by Cardijn when he said: 'Chaplains are everything and nothing'. I experienced an analogous example of that tension when I worked in East Timor for many years as an adviser to proud, newly independent but nascent

East Timorese organisations. In both settings, the idea was to do 'everything' possible to make yourself 'nothing', i.e. superfluous or at least a tomato stake not the plant.

Adults have played a critical role in Jocism from its inception and even more so in the YCS, ironically thanks to its student character. The age of its members and the nature of schooling mean there is constant turnover. In the YCS, one is always starting again both with members and young lay staff who effectively take a gap year or two to work for the YCS before resuming their education or commencing careers. Inevitably this makes the YCS particularly dependent on adults, whether chaplains, religious assistants, or, these days, laity. Experience shows that as constants and keepers of institutional memory, their presence or absence can have a decisive impact.

This fact of life is also acknowledged by IYCS. At the 1974 World Council, IYCS engaged Fr Gustavo Gutierrez as an expert and nominated Fr Ben Pelegri as international chaplain. Fathers Stan Fernando and Samuel Rayan played key roles at the Asian meeting in 1976, and Sister Jeanne Devos of India was engaged to promote YCS in the Asia-Pacific. The engagement of these clergy and religious also made clear that the IYCS continued to see itself as part of the church, informed by faith and the Christ of the gospels. Their roles, however, had been reframed in Vatican II terms, and their input recast from a Southern, not European, point of view.

Allowing that adults were an essential service in the YCS, the question was how should this service be exercised in an organisation whose purpose was the development of lay leadership. Run the show, be the expert, or king of the kids? Or, take a silent back seat and wait to be called on? Or, find a third way?

A good YCW group has a good chaplain, said Cardijn. The role is essentially to animate, advise and support, like a good sports coach, not to substitute. Our ideal assistant was the engaged adult who practised review in their own life, including with the YCS. A further quality was an adult who, as Pierre Babin put it in *Adolescents in Search of a New Church*, was prepared 'to seek faith together' with students or, to use Paulo Freire's phrase, to be a 'becoming Christian'.

This sort of thinking was a bridge too far for those with a pre-Vatican II clerical mindset. But YCS in the 1970s was blessed with the active support of some wonderful chaplains and assistants. The roll call includes priests like Bob Wilkinson, Gerry Gallagher, Mick

Byrne, Tony Stace, Wal Dethlefs, Don O'Brien, Mick Lowcock; religious like Liz Compton, Bob Trembath, Cathy Smith, Helen Foster and Meredith Evans; and laity like Peter and Marya Stewart. Their involvement was deeply valued by the national YCS and myself. Equally appreciated was the interest and support of the two bishops who successively represented YCS in the episcopal conference: Leonard Faulkner and Peter Quinn (both members of a good Committee for the Lay Apostolate that also included bishops like David Cremmin in Sydney and Philip Kennedy in Adelaide).

The role requires fine judgment and timing. It also requires a good understanding of the Gospels and church teaching, not least on the lay vocation, and ability to express this simply. Pope Francis is a master of this art. He also urges priests and religious 'to become immersed in the real lives of people' and to encourage 'freedom'. During his visit to Slovakia in September 2021, he told his audience: 'A church that has no room for the adventure of freedom, even in the spiritual life, risks becoming rigid and self-enclosed . . .. Some people may be used to this. But many others—especially the younger generations—are not attracted by a faith that leaves them no interior freedom, by a church in which all are supposed to think alike and blindly obey.' The Pope added, 'Do not be afraid to train people for a mature and free relationship with God. This approach may give the impression that we are diminishing our control, power and authority, yet the church of Christ does not seek to dominate consciences and occupy spaces but rather to be a 'wellspring' of hope in people's lives.'

Slovakia, however, is not Australia where secularism, scandals and other factors have eroded the church and where priests and religious of the type who once served the YCS as chaplains and assistants are thin on the ground. Catholic schools, however, are a conspicuous exception to this sense of diminution. Might not lay staff, for whom teaching is an expression of lay vocation, play the animating role to YCS that chaplains and religious assistants once did? Similarly, might teacher trainees be educated in Jocist principles and practice, especially in the education faculties of Catholic universities?

What did the YCS of the 70s decide about its core mission?

Basically, YCS had to decide whether secondary YCS in Australia was to be a force for institutional change in its own right or a seedbed?

The question became a dilemma following the 1974 World Conference we attended. IYCS committed the whole movement unequivocally to serve within the vanguard of change and global justice. This was fine for tertiary students and politicised young militants from the south and their northern counterparts, but out of sync with the general reality of Australian secondary school YCS. As Fr Mick Byrne observed in a letter in 1976: 'YCS is mainly secondary, struggling for an identity and a purpose, continually faced with a high turnover and the problem of developing new kids all the time'. It wasn't till the IYCS World Conference in Spain in 1978, my final year, where Kevin McDonald was elected secretary-general, that IYCS gave this situation some consideration. Australia's delegation which included grounded assistants like Sr Meredith Evans and Fr Bob Wilkinson and national personnel Frank Johnson and Dave Freeman, who was elected to the Council steering committee, did their best to make this perspective understood.

While we didn't ignore basic groups (in fact, national and diocesan staff constantly visited them around Australia), the archives show that national staff prioritised YCS leaders, regional staff and adult assistants. Representatives from these cohorts were the ones invited to national workshops, executive meetings and conferences. Our principal media, *Student Bulletin, Letter to the Executive,* and *Subscription Service* (to serious reading) carried regular apologies for being heavy. Attempts were made to lighten *Student Bulletin* with humorous cartoons, but reports from international and national conferences, chaplains' meetings, dioceses and excerpts from the life of Cardijn defied a light touch.

The records also show that national staff focused on promoting Jocist basics, including the review of life, though with a consistent emphasis on the student character of the YCS. In other words, we felt our primary role was to support those engaged in the everyday, nitty-gritty formation of students, not to ferment institutional change though, of course, we celebrated any instances of 'authentic student action'!

Our front-line stalwarts included a stellar cast of young leaders, some of them employed full-time in their localities. In no particular order and allowing for subjectivity on my part, they included: Graham Chandler (Perth), Andy Sugg (Adelaide), Annie Monsour (Brisbane), Tim Curran (Melbourne), Kath Higgins (Townsville), Mary

Harrington (George Town), Linda Baker (Perth), Mick Piotto (Adelaide), Kate McMahon (Sale), Debby Bell (Bathurst), Jenny Pritchard (Wollongong), Simone McGurk (Perth), Maryrose Hall (Ballarat), Andy Freeman (Hobart), Paula Daly (Hobart), Sharon Oates (Perth), Bern McEvoy (Adelaide), Liz Capps (Hobart), Anne Madigan (Adelaide), Carmel Fitzgerald (Brisbane), Rosie Huxtable (Hobart), Judy Dougherty (Lismore), Cathy Whewell (Adelaide), Mary Martin (Ballarat), Kim Voss (Hobart), Marianne Calleja (Perth), Peter Gartlan (Launceston), Tony O'Gorman (Brisbane), Shawn Boyle (Perth), Jenny Pritchard (Wollongong), Chris Keating (Perth), Marg Crowley (Bathurst), Mick Burstow (Brisbane), Kath Kelsey (Adelaide), Karen Chandler (Bathurst), and Therese McLean (Maitland).

Our focus on fundamentals was kicked on significantly by the next generation of national YCS. That is, by the end of decade, Australian YCS had decided it was fundamentally a 'seedbed'. By then, national YCS had re-located from Fitzroy to the YCW office in Lonsdale St, Melbourne, an arrangement that facilitated useful interaction with National YCW and the Melbourne YCS and YCW who also used it as their base.

David Freeman and Sister Elizabeth Compton, with input from Mick Piotto, were responsible for this initiative. Each had many years of hands-on YCS experience (in Tasmania and Adelaide respectively, both places that had long Jocist traditions). Dave had attended the 1978 IYCS World Council in Valladolid, Spain, and Liz Compton was a former assistant, teacher and principal well versed in YCS, schools and teaching method. With the support of the national executive, they revived the handbook.

A staple of YCS in its first three decades, the handbook had been ditched after Vatican II in favour of a more self-generated, situational, less top-down approach. But, as Fr Mick Byrne had pointed out in 1976, secondary YCS, like it or not, is 'faced with a high turnover and the problem of developing new kids all the time'. The new resource book would address this recurring need. 'There was a widespread feeling that something was needed', wrote the authors in their foreword, 'and there were many requests . . . we wanted to write something that helped people gradually discover the YCS, but which also left the thinking and decisions in the hands of each group'.

Published in 1981, the outcome, drafted by Dave Freeman, test driven by groups and finessed over three years, comprised three kits:

YCS Resource Kit (resource book plus leaflets); *YCS Leaders Kit* (leaders/assistants book plus articles); *YCS Assistants Kit* (book, review of life booklet, articles). The kits were a creative blend of the old and the new. Group dynamics, structures, methods and the role of leaders and assistants were addressed. But so too were the emphases and insights of the 1970s: Vatican II, Cardijn's vision, the centrality of Christ and the Gospels, review of life, action, reflection and engagement with the world, including the global village.

They had prepared a seedbed that, composted with the wisdom of decades, they hoped would yield a rich harvest. A bit like the grain of wheat on the YCS logo.

That's all pretty serious. What about the joy bit you mentioned at the start?

It was a thrill, if not a joy, to associate with icons like Paulo Freire and Gustavo Gutierrez, to

travel and attend the IYCS conference in 1974, the 1976 regional meeting in Thailand (where we were caught up in Thailand's latest military coup), and to plug into Latin America, a most exciting place politically and theologically, now refreshingly represented in the Vatican itself. There was also a lot of fun in the communal experiment at 528 Brunswick St, Fitzroy.

I also got satisfaction from helping produce our various media. We professionalised *Student Bulletin,* which had been started before me in 1973, making it into a substantial and readable regular news and information publication. Working with the Dominican *Bulletin of Christian Affairs* in Canberra, we also published an innovative series of five simplified church documents for lay and student readers. With discussion questions at the end, they included: *Justice in the World* (Synod Bishops, 1971); *The Church and the Modern World* (Vatican II); *The Progress of Peoples* (Pope John XXIII); *The Apostolate of the Laity* (Vatican II). The initiative was welcomed outside the YCS as well, and led to orders from overseas, including the US.

My best memory though is of my YCS colleague 'fulltimers'. I can't help thinking of them now without admiration, respect, an affectionate chuckle and pride in what they've individually achieved since YCS days, though sadly not Mick Perkins, who died in 1976 as mentioned. Though theoretically engaged by the Bishops conference, they certainly didn't live like bishops (or want to, of course). They made do on a very meagre income, lived simply, sharing accommodation, chores and bills, spending any extra money on books, leaving little time or resources for shows and sport. Though they didn't see it this way, they effectively gave up one or two years to share their ideals, vision, and experience with students in the hope their work would contribute to the church and the world. But, as I've indicated, this work wasn't all wine and roses.

These colleagues were Mick Perkins (1973–1974). Kevin McDonald (1973–1974), Damian Hurley (1974–1975), Lorna Payne (1976–1977), Frank Johnson (1977–1979), and David Freeman (1978–1979). All blokes, I note, except one, interesting given the preponderance of young women at the local level in my list above. We spent a lot of time together; some of it in monastic silence, unproductive reflection, cleaning our pipes or seemingly endless analysis; all of it in camaraderie. They make a happy note to end on!

Pat Walsh, September 2021

YCS in the 1970s and 1980s

Linda Baker

I was born in 1959, the last year of the baby boomers, growing up in the sixties and seventies. I joined a YCS school group in early 1975, which was the year I turned sixteen, and is what we would now call year eleven. I attended Mercedes School for Girls in Perth, and the school was in the city, next to Victoria Square. In the middle of the Square was the Perth Catholic Cathedral, and across the road from the Cathedral was the Bishop's Palace and the Catholic Church offices, where the YCS full-timer was based. Suffice to say I found myself geographically in the thick of it regarding both the YCS and the Catholic Church.

1975 was a year that oscillated between the radical 60's and the greedy 80's, and in my experience, young people of time did the same. After two years as a member of my school YCS group, I was a YCS full-timer in Perth in 1977 and 1978, and a national full-timer in 1979 and 1980, and I was Australian YCS President in 1980. This gave me a longer than usual YCS perspective as most people were full-timers for a maximum of two years.

Punk music and disco were taking over from the folk singers of the sixties, and the world was becoming a little more hedonistic than earlier times.

The Church of the time of my YCS involvement from 1975 to 1980, was coming out of the post-Vatican II era, and very gradually becoming resolved in the need for change, however little, and however slowly. This work was led by Pope Paul IV and his efforts to continue the work and changes emerging from Vatican II, and Pope John XXIII's vision for the Church.

By the late seventies, Sunday mass numbers were noticeably tapering off, less men were becoming priests, less women were becoming nuns, talk of married priests and women priests was brewing, and before we knew it, we had Pope John Paul II, and his steady, systemic move away from Vatican II and away from anchoring the Church in the modern world.

In a nutshell, in his twenty-six years as Pope from 1978 to 2005, Pope John Paul II did many things, and one particular thing he did, I believe fundamentally changed the Church. He created 231 cardinals who were mostly conservative men. The perspective on this is best understood when it is compared to the 112 cardinals that existed in 1978 when he took office (numbers from Wikkipedia). It is worth noting that as the number of cardinals more than doubled, the number of priests and lay people's attendance at Mass each Sunday was severely declining. Therefore, what was the need for so many more cardinals, especially conservative ones, other than to more easily exert control over the Vatican and the Church?

A rudimentary understanding of politics confirms that power always come down to numbers, and 231 conservative cardinals would have a major impact on Church decisions during the years of Pope John Paul II's reign. Whatever the motivation of Pope John Paul II and the Vatican of his time, it would seem obvious to be a lot easier to create the voting cardinals you may want, rather than changing the minds of the existing cardinals you inherited.

He also ex-communicated several theologians, including some from the ranks of the liberation theologians and the mystic theologians. During this time the focus of the Church moved further towards anti-abortion, anti-homosexuality, anti-women priests, and anti-married priests. This focus was not always followed by members of the Church.

These actions were among the factors that would result in the fabric of the Church changing, moving from expansion to contraction. The juggernaut of the Catholic Church, steered by Pope John Paul II and the Vatican, moved away from the beginnings of the openness, collaboration and promise of Vatican II.

These changes came from the top of the Catholic Church and were fed down to the bottom of the organisation, not the other way round. This could go some way to explaining why the actions of this pope did not ultimately succeed, if success is measured by numbers of people identifying as Catholic, going to Mass on Sundays and putting money in the collection plate. In my experience, most organisations do not measure their success by a significant and continuing loss of membership and the funds provided by that membership.

Forty years later, we can see the result. Few Catholic lay people going to Mass on Sundays, and almost none of these people are below thirty-five years old; practically no nuns, brothers and priests teaching in Catholic schools; very few priests; local churches and parishes closing; and a unified and clear vision of the future of the Catholic Church is not easy to observe in Australia. (Please note trends are sometimes different in developing countries).

Somewhere in the mix are the cases of sexual abuse by Church leaders of Catholic children and women. Interestingly, when I read the list of excommunications during the time of Pope John Paul II, I saw no people on the list where the reason given was that they abused children or women. I did see that one poor teenage girl under eighteen was excommunicated for having an abortion after being found pregnant after she was raped. (details from Wikipedia)

It is too simple to say that Pope John Paul II's actions solely have caused the much-reduced numbers attending mass, however I believe it is a significant factor in the changes of the Church in recent times.

The secular politics of the time moved from Gough Whitlam's time as the fastest moving policy maker and bringer of change in Australian political history, to the Malcolm Fraser years of business expansion, growth of the big banks and financial institutions, and laws against student unionisms in our universities. The eighties was a time of closing down the education opportunities that Whitlam had opened up to Australians. It was definitely the end of the sixties era of change, and the beginning of the eighties era of greed, with a muddle of a no man's land in between.

This was the political landscape, the Church environment and Australian culture surrounding me during my YCS involvement between 1975 and 1980.

We were not a parish-oriented family. Dad was a Catholic and mum was a non-church going Presbyterian. Dad would take us to Mass on Sunday and we would arrive late, sit down the back of the Church, and leave directly after communion. We would go to a variety of churches and were not members of any particular parish. We believed in God and did not object to going to Mass on Sunday, but we had little to nothing to do with a parish.

Even though my parents were members of different Christian religions, the Catholic Church was the only church we knew. None of us ever got to the bottom of exactly what a Presbyterian was, and to this day I have not set foot in a Presbyterian church—by circumstance, not design.

At school I was a 'joiner-in', and I had been a 'joiner-in' my whole life. I was a student leader in my school, mostly by default, as not everyone joined in things to the degree I did. In kindergarten my mother told me that I would volunteer to bring the dress-ups home for her to wash each weekend (this did not impress her). In grade one I was the conductor of the grade one band, and I was the Arithmetic Girl, back in the days when we used the word 'arithmetic'. In grade seven I was a school captain and captain of the Red sports team, which amused my father as he thought I was lousy at sport. By year eleven I had been president of the school debating club for two years, I played netball, volunteered for fund raising projects, and pretty much joined in most school activities.

In the past I have wondered what specifically appealed to me about the YCS. At its core, I believe it was the desire in me to make a positive difference in what was often a harsh world, where I mostly felt rendered powerless. The message of the YCS was that change through See-Judge-Act was possible.

The little I knew about YCS was that it had a focus on justice, change, a belief in God, and a general desire to make the world a better place. I understood that this was done through action. I learnt that this was called the 'mission' of the YCS. This appealed to me because, like many teenagers, I hated unfair things, and, like many teenagers, I had a long list of what I believed were unfair things.

I wanted to talk about these issues and nut things out, but more importantly, I really, really wanted to act on them to create change. The YCS's focus on personal and collective action for change greatly appealed to me and came at a time when I was ready to become involved in such action.

I joined the school YCS group, and I went to the meetings. I doubt I would have joined a group focused on singing at mass, or putting on church nativity plays, or a bible study group, as at that time, these things would not have held my interest. YCS offered a focus on justice and the chance to do something to change things, and that definitely held my attention.

As the Perth YCS full-timer (Sharon Oates) was based across the road from my school, she often made an appearance at our meetings. During the meetings we looked for issues or events that were either unjust, unfair, wrong, or just plain bad, and we worked out ways to make them right. I was hooked from the start.

So it began for me, and I immediately galvanized into action. It was like a door to a new way of living had been opened where we could *actually* change the world, not just talk about it. For someone in a school where we used to get demerit points for having our long socks drooped below the knee to the ankle, YCS actions seemed infinitely more meaningful. I felt that this was what I had been looking for—a real chance to make a real difference; a difference in me, in my surroundings, in the Church, and in the world. I saw the YCS's mission and the Church's mission as the same, even if it did not always look the same.

We found all manner of things that we thought needed changing, from apartheid in South Africa; to the school's archaic debutante ball that we deemed sexist; to the way some exams were done unfairly in the school's history department; to changing the school uniform, and much more. When Gough Whitlam was sacked a few of us from our school YCS group took it upon ourselves to get this talked about in our classes, not just in the playground.

We learnt the See – Judge – Act method, often referred to in the student movements as See – Reflect – Act, or the Review of Life method. In later years, some members referred to it as praxis, but I always felt it embodied more than praxis. We saw that the actions needed to be based on something greater than an emotional response to a particular situation. This appealed to me, as it seemed to remove frivolous thinking and a lack of depth or lack of analysis from our focus and our actions.

We went on YCS camps, had endless meetings, and in general, we created a community of students who mostly wanted to contribute something more than was expected of them. We caught up with students from other groups, saw them on weekends, and several of us became YCS leaders and good friends.

In Perth and some WA country areas such as Bunbury, New Norcia, and Geraldton, there were probably twenty or so YCS groups. They were mostly school based, though some parishes had YCS groups too. Groups sizes varied from five or six to around twenty-five students, and overall, there were probably 250–300 students in WA that attended YCS group meetings on a reasonably regular basis.

The structure of YCS in Western Australia was simple. There were YCS groups, and the leaders of these groups would go to executive meetings, which were essentially leaders' meetings. Each WA diocese operated separately regarding their leadership meetings, although many camps and meetings included students from several dioceses.

We also voted for students to represent us nationally at the Australian level of the YCS. There was a strict boundary, particularly at national meetings whereby students rather than fulltime YCS workers or YCS chaplains and adult assistants, were allowed to vote on resolutions. Sometimes, especially at the national level, there were deep divisions, which I later recognised were the same type of divisions seen in the factions that were evident in student politics and Australian political parties, essentially the difference between left and right thinking.

Voting rights and issues to be voted on, could sometimes be hazy, but one thing was clear—YCS was a student movement, and although groups embraced full-timers and adult chaplains or assistants, at the executive level and national level, only students voted.

To be a chaplain or assistant to a YCS group, or a YCS diocese, was only for those priests, nuns or teachers made of sturdy stuff, as the natural way for most priests was to be in charge, to be followed, or to be a vocal and respected adviser. At YCS meetings they could not vote, and this did not always sit well with chaplains. Those that were comfortable in this environment were wonderful, and very supportive of students, chaplains and assistants such as Father Pat Walsh, Sister Meredith Evans, Brother Kevin Johns (a Christian brother from Perth), Father Bob Wilkinson, Father Tom Gleeson, and the wonderful Father Hugh O'Sullivan, to name a few.

We all liked the idea of action, however when the time came to *actually* act, not everyone in the group wanted to be front and centre or go as far as others who wanted to take the action. For some, self-preservation kicked in, while for others like me, the desire to forge ahead no matter what, was upper most in my mind. These experiences taught me that when you get to the skinny branches, the air is thinner, and the people are fewer. Sometimes with certain difficult actions, I felt like Frodo from Lord of the Rings, crawling up the impossible mountain all on my own.

An example of this was the YCS Campaign Against Apartheid in South Africa. This began when a YCW full-timer in South Africa was imprisoned. After an examination of the situation through the review of life process, we believed that Apartheid needed to end, and that all adult people in South Africa should have the right to vote. A core group of about eight to ten of us talked, planned, and took action. Using the Cardijn principle of it being better to get ten people to do the work of one, rather than one person to do the work of ten, we involved as many other students as possible, even if they could only come to a few events or meetings.

These actions included educating ourselves by reading and seeking out organisations to inform us such as the Campaign Against Racial Exploitation (CARE). We organised for CARE's representative to give talks at schools and churches and we acquired literature from them. We organised protests outside Sunday Masses at the Cathedral, and created educational materials to give people coming to mass. We gave talks at schools and churches. We wrote articles for school newsletters and the Catholic Diocesan Press. These actions took place over a period of months, and we were very passionate about it.

What we had not expected, was that these actions would produce such a reaction in the Perth Catholic community. Naively, we though that wanting to end Apartheid was a no brainer, an obvious position for a decent person to agree with and want. We thought that no-one in Perth would disagree, even if they did not want to do anything, as Apartheid was so easily recognized as anti-democratic and so destructive.

What I know now that I didn't know then, is that outside South Africa, the highest population of white South Africans in the world is found in Perth. Most of these people were in Perth because they agreed with Apartheid, and wanted to live in a white community, with a strong economy and a similar climate to South Africa, In the seventies and early eighties, they left South Africa in large numbers as it was clear that Apartheid was crumbling.

We were attacked in the Catholic press, and many of the attacks became increasingly vitriolic. We were accused of being Communists, of siding with criminals, of being anti-Catholic, of being ignorant and stupid, and of being anti-Australian. These attacks appeared every week in the Catholic press, and each week they became worse. Some students became scared, and some supporters buckled under this pressure.

We felt abandoned, and we could not really understand why there was such viciousness in the attacks. We were at a loss as to what to do to continue our action yet stop the attacks. We were fortunate to have a strong supporter who helped us enormously.

I will be forever grateful to the YCS Episcopal Vicar of the time, the Perth Auxiliary Bishop, Peter Quinn. Prior to this campaign, Bishop Quinn was familiar with the YCS and had attended several Perth meetings and national executive meetings. He couldn't believe we worked until late in the night at our meetings. He said even the bishops didn't work this long at their meetings, and he said that sometimes he wanted to ask could he go to bed earlier than us, but he thought that would be bad form, and he should stay as we worked late into the night.

Bishop Quinn liked young people and offered them encouragement. He would occasionally come over to our house for dinner, and I don't mean a nice family dinner cooked by mum. I mean a lousy serve of spaghetti bolognaise or tuna mornay cooked by some seventeen and eighteen-year-olds in a share household, pre-MasterChef sensibilities. Looking back, I think he smoked so much after dinner to get the taste out of his mouth.

Suffice to say, Bishop Quinn, who didn't mind it if we called him Peter, put up with a lot, and was always, even under pressure, a great supporter of the YCS and young people.

It became clear after about three weeks of our anti-Apartheid campaign that the attacks on us in the Catholic press were escalating in both number and tone. Without any request from us, Bishop Quinn wrote a letter in support of the YCS and in support of our actions to promote the end to Apartheid. He talked about how young we were, how few of us there were, and how we were motivated by goodness, not hate or power. He questioned why decent Catholic people would attack us instead of supporting us or praising us. He talked about the YCS as a valuable Catholic organisation for forming young people. In short, he said the attacks on us had to stop.

To our amazement, we were never attacked again in the Catholic press over this campaign.

We were very happy, but more than that, we were very relieved. We were too young to have a thick skin, or reasonable insight into how predictable it was for us to be targeted if we took the type of actions we did. We were supported in this action by the national

YCW full-timer of the time, Michael Campbell, who came to work in Perth during my first year as a full-timer. Michael and his wife Lesley were knowledgeable and generous in teaching us so much about Cardijn, the Review of Life method and how to be better organised.

Several years later when I was at university, I came across the organiser for CARE (Campaign Against Racial Exploitation) and thanked him for all the support he gave a bunch of kids like us during that YCS anti-Apartheid campaign, and for the many talks he gave at catholic schools and churches. His feedback was that he was glad to do anything to raise awareness about Apartheid as he was a Jew from South Africa and had seen firsthand the damage Apartheid had caused. He also told me he was a Communist, which I had not known previously. I laughed at the irony of us—in ignorance—organising a communist to speak at our Catholic schools and parishes. If only our attackers at that time knew!

These actions, and our discussions in the YCS meetings were focussed on our 'mission', which was to change the world into a better place, and to correct injustice where we found it. We consciously used the word 'mission', as we felt we had a personal mission, that the YCS had its mission, and the Church had a mission. We were always trying to align these missions, somewhat naively.

My years as a National YCS full-timer were different to my time as a WA full-timer, and I was based in Melbourne for two years. The national job required lengthy visits to various dioceses to work with YCS groups and leaders. The dioceses I visited were mostly in NSW, and mainly in Sydney where the YCS was newer and less established than elsewhere. This work could be lonely and isolating, and some previous full-timers based in Melbourne were very welcoming, such as Mark Considine and his wife Gen Timmins and their families.

During the second year as a national full-timer, I lived in the YCW house in Melbourne with the YCW full-timers, and we also worked in the YCW building in Lonsdale Street in Melbourne. The YCW full-timers Stefan Gigacz and Terry Byrne were always up for discussions about how to improve the world, and what full-timers could do to encourage YCS and YCW groups to develop leaders and their actions. During this time, I met some YCW full-timers from Adelaide, Bernie McEvoy and Denis Byrne, and others who had been YCS members including the Regan family—Anthony, Madeleine, Frances, and Hilary. All of these people had a positive impact on me during those years, with many being good friends today.

One of the things that we did as national full-timers, was to simplify some of the documents emanating from Vatican II, such as The Church in the Modern World (sometimes referred to as The Pastoral Constitution on the Church in the Modern World) and the Decree on the Apostolate of the Laity. This was done as a way for students to become educated about Vatican II and the direction of the church. We believed if we simplified and shortened the texts, they would be more likely to be read by young people. It was a direct link between the YCS and the Catholic Church, and we wanted that link. We saw ourselves and the YCS as part of the church, even when we were frustrated with the Church.

During these years I also attended several Australian Bishops meetings (The Australian Episcopal Conference), where we explained what we did and sought continued funding from the bishops. We also attended some national meetings of priests, often with bishops in attendance. These meetings could be daunting and mystifying. The bishops' meetings were very formal, not so much the priests' meetings.

During my time, we were treated well by these groups, and I felt there was an understanding of the importance of the Cardijn youth movements by the church leadership, even when we frustrated them. I did not however, like our dependence on the Church for funding, and understood it could be withdrawn at any time, very much to our detriment. We had some champions of the youth movements among the bishops of the time, such as Bishop Leonard Faulkner, Bishop Peter Quinn and Archbishop Jimmy Gleeson.

I know there is some debate as to whether the YCS is a 'movement'. I will leave that discussion to the academics among us. Whether the youth movements are deemed 'movements' in the pure sense or not, is not a question which particularly interests me. What I find far more interesting, is witnessing and continuing to discover the impact the YCS and its members had and continue to have on their workplace, their communities and the church.

Many lay people who became Church leaders after my time in the YCS had a background in the Cardijn based youth movements. In general terms, these people often functioned to question the church, to promote and generate progressive causes within the Church, to promote lay people within the church, and to involve the Church in the world outside the church. A pertinent example is the Circle of Friends organisation, which supports refugees living within our community here in Adelaide. Sister Meredith Evans who co-ordinates this group is a Mercy nun and former YCS assistant, and this is a group of mainly Catholics, with many members such as me, who are former YCS or YCW leaders.

From the small group of YCS leaders I worked with in Perth several went on to become YCS full-timers, locally and nationally, and we were later involved in student politics together when we attended the University of Western Australia. Some of these students were Dave Kelly and Simone McGurk, who are both are currently minsters in the WA parliament, and Shawn Boyle, who was CEO of WACOSS (WA Council of Social Services). Other YCS leaders and members that I knew and worked with in Perth, have gone into politics, unions, and social justice organisations. Several have worked in poverty-stricken countries such as Nicaragua, or the Philippines, and several including myself, have worked internationally in refugee camps or for NGO's overseas.

During my university years, I became the Western Australian State Organiser for the Australian Union of Students (AUS) which was a fulltime job, and on a monthly basis I attended executive meetings at AUS headquarters in Lygon Street in Melbourne. In the early eighties student unions were under attack with anti-union legislation in both Western Australia and Queensland, and we ran campaigns to try and overturn such legislation. Almost all the people at these AUS executive meetings went into politics or unions, including Julie Gillard and my good friend Gayle Tierney who is a minster in the Victorian Parliament. My AUS work was a direct result of what I had learned in YCS.

However, I think the great gift of the Cardijn youth movements is the development of leaders, who are today still leaders and taking action in the communities they find themselves in, however grand or humble. The mission of taking action in our lives, in the places we work, the places we have friends and families, and the causes we see as important, is where we continue to be involved and participate for the improvement of people's circumstances.

After my time in YCS, in my mid-twenties, I worked for Greg Crafter, a minster in the South Australian parliament, who had previously been a YCW full-timer. I was referred to Greg by Brian Moylan, who had been the worker for Adult Family Groups in the Adelaide church and was a previous YCW leader. My trainer and boss in Greg's office was Sue King, who before my time had been a YCS leader in Adelaide. I found that the links, skills, and methods forged by the YCS and YCW were strong and provided a base line understanding of an individual, even in environments where that may not be clear for others.

Greg Crafter taught me that leadership is service, and all of us in that political office used what we had learnt in our time in the Cardijn youth movements to continue to work in such a way to improve the world we are in, whatever we were doing. We are still friends and catch up regularly and enjoy discussing the variety of things we are doing, such as Greg Crafter being involved in getting the Elgin Marbles returned to Greece.

In my experience and observation, the training of the YCS has stayed with me and many, many others, for years afterwards. The YCS training we received has continued to contribute to the good in the world and the church through the way we do our jobs, interact with people and strive for positive change.

YCS was not a single focus organization, rather it was a training ground and inspiration for young people to take action in their lives, and to develop a solid link between faith and the world. For many, that also applied to the church. Most YCS members left when they were about seventeen or eighteen, with a few working for two years as a full-timer after that. We were too young to be leading the revolution, but the seeds were sown in our small group meetings, our relationships with each other, and our desire to learn.

So many YCS members went on to do to all manner of extraordinary things, in the environments and circumstances they found themselves in. You will find previous YCS members on school committees, in parish councils, on sports committees, as sport coaches, in unions, in political parties, in parliament, in businesses, in self help groups, in the arts, and in community organizations.

YCS trained young people to be leaders, to have a process—See-Judge-Act—that allowed them to take actions rather than blindly react to injustices. The review of life method also helped to develop understanding, create actions, and the consequent understanding of the impact of those actions, and any necessary subsequent actions.

The leaders and leadership qualities developed by the YSC in its members, and their continuing influence on the world is the legacy of the YCS, whether it is defined as a movement or not. It would be difficult to find an organization that trained a relatively small number of people who have continued to spread themselves out into the world with such a large and positive impact.

This is such a significant thing. It is the great gift of the YCS to its members, to the church and most importantly, to the world. It is the gift of the YCS to me, for which I will be forever grateful.

Cardijn Studies: On the Church in the World of Today: Volume 4/1 2023

The Student Movement and the YCS in the Early 1970s

Mark Considine and Anthony J Regan

Introduction

One of the things that made the social movement work so important to many of us was the deep and enduring connections we felt to one another and the optimism that working together could generate. More than fifty years later many of the threads and connections remain. We shared many of these same experiences and so we decided to write about them together.

1. Mark's memories of key events

One of many memories that remain hard-wired from my two years as a national fulltime worker was a road trip from Melbourne to Sydney in early 1972 with FR KJ Smith and Tim Walsh. KJ was national chaplain for the YCW and Tim was National President. We were heading up to the national bishop's conference to attend the annual meeting of the sub-committee charged with responsibility for the lay apostolate. In practical terms this meant oversight of the YCW and the YCS, each of which received funding to assist with the costs of running their national offices, both located in Melbourne. KJ was one of the classic Cardijn priests of that era who spoke truth to power and supported young people to take a strong place in both church and society. For reasons discussed below, the YCS was without a national chaplain in 1972, so he was also helping us navigate church politics and hold onto our funding.

The sub-committee included about ten bishops as I recall, each of whom attended in full regalia of long black soutane with wide red belt and matching skull-cap. They were an impressive, even intimidating sight. They sat in a circle and a spare chair was waiting for me when my turn arrived to give a report and be questioned. They were well aware that the happy, prayerful YCS groups of the past were being extended by activist young leaders wanting to question things. After reporting that our numbers were up and our work was going well, I paused for questions. One of the older bishops led the charge. 'We have heard about this Little Red School Book that is circulating in some parishes. Apparently it wants our young people to become followers of Mao Tse Tung. Listening to your report I get the impression you think the same?'

I began explaining that the book in question was actually written by two Danish school teachers, and was quickly interrupted, 'Lutherans then'. That was the end of the Little Red School Book discussion. No more needed to be said evidently. A further half hour of testy questions and gratuitous interruptions made it clear that we had work to do in making our case. I tried to explain to them that many of the things the YCS had always sought to do, including calling young people to action and supporting their desire to have an impact on issues that concerned them, was now also being felt in a broader student movement with a wide array of political agendas influenced by the social changes of the 1960s.

Thinking about that meeting now I am more impressed than I think I was at the time. I had left the discussion aware only of our differences and their evident hostility. My powers of persuasion had yielded no points of sympathy. But now, looking back, I feel the account was probably more evenly balanced. They had asked exactly the questions we could have expected and by registering concern they forced us to be clearer about what was special about our approach to social action. And after all, they kept funding us.

2. What were we attempting to say?

This was not our last debate with the bishops nor our only point of tension with the organised church of the day, but it was emblematic. We were working at a time when the tectonic plates of church and society were shifting. We were doing our part to have a view about that shift and to encourage students to get involved. But to get to that issue we need to first go back a step. As I am sure other accounts in this volume will have attested, the YCS of the 1960s was a different beast to the one that emerged in the early 1970s.

My involvement started in 1969 while at school at Monivae College, then an all-boys school in western Victoria. Fr Pat Walsh, who also has a chapter in this volume, was a young priest and teacher at the school and was given the role as chaplain to the day scholars in a school dominated by its much larger boarding population. We 'day scrags' were the bottom of the pecking order and many of us soon enjoyed the opportunity which the YCS afforded to get organised. With Pat's extraordinary gift for guidance, we soon had three groups going and before long we also had a group at the local high school.

The focus of the movement in this period was the development of leadership and the idea that by reflecting upon the experiences of our lives as students we could identify ways in which we could each make things better. The 'better' in most cases was local and personal. It included helping someone in need, or calling out our own poor behaviour, or reflecting on the individual pressures we felt growing up, doing exams and figuring out what to do next. Sometimes we even talked about girls.

But it also had an undeclared ideal which would grow larger and become more explicit in the next couple of years. This was the experience that students in organised groups, with leaders of their own, felt as a form of identity and solidarity, a sense of being joined to something bigger and something purposeful. Probably none of us would have put it in these terms back then, but the practical manifestations were striking. The numbers joining groups expanded rapidly. Mini-conferences and training days drawing students from across the region were equally popular and soon saw networks forming with schools in neighbouring cities. Undoubtedly the high-point of these wider experiences were the annual summer schools run in Ballarat and bringing fifty to sixty students together to discuss and debate the big issues of the day.

At the end of 1970, having just finished final year at school, and with all the certainties and vague curiosities of a seventeen-year old kid from the country, I left home to become a fulltime member of the national team. Looking back I wonder what that young man thought he was doing. I knew none of the other team members and knew little of the work that fulltime organisers did. But it felt like a serious adventure, something important that did not (yet) involve a bigger decision about what to do with my life.

The national office was on level three of Cathedral Hall in Fitzroy. Downstairs was the Confraternity of Christian Doctrine (CCD), an off-putting bit of church terminology that described the interesting work of chaplains and nuns who went into state schools to provide support and teach the Christian message. Their leader was the amazing Fr Tom Doyle who would become an important ally.

On our floor were the offices of the long-time national chaplain, Fr Paul Kane; national president Sue Carman; the other new full-time national organiser, Liz Whitehouse; a new post for the fulltime worker in regional Victoria, Trev Bate; the movement's administrator, Lorraine Walsh, the Melbourne full timer, Margaret Molony and me. Fr Kane had been chaplain for many years and held the history of the organisation in his head. He was energetic and effective in managing a wide network of priests and nuns who were the traditional backbone of the organisation. Sue was in her third year as a fulltime worker and was both inspiring and supportive to all those around her.

3. Anthony as Adelaide 'full-timer', 1970–1971

I belonged to a small YCS group for my last two years of high school in Adelaide, 1968 and 1969, at all male Blackfriars Priory School, run by the generally conservative Dominican priests. The YCS group was conducted in a desultory fashion, notionally advised by a priest who did not show a great deal of interest. So we generally attempted to run the meetings ourselves, though I remember very little of them other than not being too clear about what we should be doing. I cannot even recall clearly why I first joined. Perhaps in part it was because outside of the class-room, school life was dominated by the sports-focussed boys, every out-of-class minute devoted to cricket or basketball in summer, and kicking footballs back and forth between similar aged groups in winter. I was a clumsy youth, with no football, cricket, or basketball prowess, or interest, and so sat low in the school's social hierarchy. Though I can't be sure, I'd assume most of the few that attended YCS meetings were similarly placed. So perhaps YCS offered a place for us, and a loose network to belong to.

There was, perhaps, another factor. I was one of seven children in a deeply Catholic family, politically conservative. My parents voted for and talked openly about support for the goals of the Democratic Labour Party (DLP), though it's popular support in South Australia was weak. In my early to mid-teens, with siblings, I handed out DLP how-to-vote cards for a local accountant who stood in a series of elections, despite knowing—as I only realised later—that he would never gain more than a tiny percentage of votes. The family interest in politics sat beside both some concerns about inequality, and an emphasis on attempting to 'do good' in life, on a personal level. By my second year with the YCS, as I learnt more about how it was expected to operate, I think that the 'review of life' part of the formulaic YCS meeting program interested me, as encouraging both 'good works' and reflection on a person's own behaviour towards others. But for the time being, I did not see it as going much beyond that.

In 1969, I became leader of the little Blackfriars YCS group. It was not a particularly sought-after role, and so It's likely that I volunteered for the job rather than being either elected by the group, or appointed by the nominal chaplain. The role did involve attending Adelaide Archdiocese group leader's meetings, and at one of the first of these that I went to, early in 1969, I unexpectedly got elected to the YCS diocesan 'team', I thinks as a representative of YCS groups from the north of Adelaide. The team was a group of eight (I think), Dennis Moore (later a well-known actor) as president. We were actively encouraged and supported by long-time archdiocese chaplain, Fr Barrymore Hynes. We met regularly (perhaps monthly?), and were encouraged to have contact with leaders of YCS groups in the areas we nominally represented, and helped conduct the occasional 'training day', and I think a training weekend or two held at the YCW training centre at Stirling, in the Adelaide hills. I enjoyed the contact with the council members, another new network of vaguely like-minded people.

There had never been a 'full-timer' working for the YCS in Adelaide, and as far as I recall my introduction to the concept came in the middle of 1969 when two 'full-timers', members of the then 'national team', Elizabeth Proust, and Suzanne (Sue) Carman, visited Adelaide for a few days. They met with the diocesan team, and I think we probably had other contact. They impressed me as highly intelligent and thoughtful people, trying to make a little difference in the world. That network was still expanding.

At that point, I was not too clear what I should do on completing high school, beyond being clear that I wanted to go to university. My three older siblings had all taken that path, and their university friends were around our house in my last few years at school, and what was discussed certainly helped open my eyes. My father, a long-time Australian army warrant officer, sometimes struggled with the new directions in which the thinking and action of his children were going. My uncertainty about my future led to discussions with my parents, and I was a bit horrified at my father's suggestion over the washing up one night that I consider joining the army. Beyond assuming I'd do tertiary study, I had vague ideas of doing some sort of education on industrial relations, thinking that might equip me to 'do good' for 'the workers'!

I cannot now recall the detail of emergence, in the second half of 1969, of discussion of the possibility of funding being provided (by the Adelaide Archdiocese, I think) to enable employment of Adelaide's first YCS 'full-timer'. There was enthusiastic discussion of the idea in the diocesan team, but little attention to what such a person would actually 'do'. I was very surprised one day when our chaplain, Fr Hynes, took me aside and suggested that I apply for the job. When I got over the considerable shock at his suggestion, I realised that it interested me as an extension of the little 'good work' the YCS involvement had encouraged me to attempt in the previous two years. At the same time I doubted that I could ever possibly operate at the impressive level that I felt that the national level full-timers achieved. The one-year appointment on offer would also give me a break from study, and perhaps give me some time to consider more what I should do with my adult life. Luckily, the Commonwealth Scholarship covering university fees and living allowance that I was offered at the end of year 12 could be deferred for twelve months.

Several people applied for the job, and an interview panel was assembled, led by Fr Hynes. Amongst the questions asked were some relating to my knowledge of the 'Catholic Faith', and I felt that I did not do at all well in the interview. So I was surprised to be offered the job, starting in January 1970, on what seemed to me the generous salary of $32 per week. In preparation for the job, in December 1969, I attended what I think was called the annual national 'key leader's' week. Held in Ocean Grove, southwest of Melbourne, it was attended by forty or fifty student leaders, most about to enter final year of high school the following year. Amongst the students attending was Mark Considine, who impressed me as a quiet, intense and thoughtful person. The event was largely organised by full-timers Brian Lawrence and Sue Carman, together with national chaplain, Fr Kane. I particularly remember my first meeting with Brian for the strong piece of initial advice he offered: 'Don't learn to type!' (for apparently that would somehow divert a man from more important work!). It was undoubtedly one of the worst pieces of advice that I—unfortunately—ever accepted, and Brian has agreed with me in that regard!

The key leader's week was my first experience of the quite high and infectious level of intensity that accompanied the various categories of YCS national-level meetings and training sessions. They brought together many mainly highly intelligent and focused young people, many of them questioning various aspects of the world, from within the relative safety of a supportive Catholic community.

I ended up working as the Adelaide full-timer not for one, but for two years, January 1970 to December 1971. It's difficult to remember in any detail how my time was occupied, day to day. There were the regular diocesan team meetings, Trevor Bate being one of its members in 1970. There were one day and weekend 'training' meetings or weekend workshops at Stirling. I visited and talked with members of many of the fifty or sixty YCS groups in various parts of Adelaide and nearby areas, and some quite a distance from Adelaide. For example, at least twice I went the 436 kilometres by road to Mount Gambier, staying in the Catholic 'deanery', dominated by elderly and conservative Dean Travers, who not only paid no attention to his young guest, but also did not seem to warm much to his curate, Hugh O'Sullivan, a long-time and committed YCW chaplain who was also very supportive of the YCS. I started a monthly or two-monthly YCS magazine, which I think lasted only a year. Students from various YCS groups would drop by my office in the afternoons after school, to talk more about life generally than YCS matters. I had semi-regular contact with the YCS national team members, mainly Fr Kane and Sue Carman. I went to Melbourne a few times to meet them, and I think that there were one or two visits from them to Adelaide. I was surprised, late in 1970, to be advised by Fr Kane that I was to read a prayer of the faithful at a Papal visit youth mass in November 1970, attended by tens of thousands, in Sydney, at the Randwick race course.

I worked in a little office that Fr Hynes organised (and had freshly painted) for me in the slightly dilapidated two story building I recall being referred to as the 'diocesan building', next to the Adelaide cathedral. I developed good relationships with others working or regularly visiting that building. They included Fr Bob Wilkinson ('Wilko'), then editor of the weekly Catholic newspaper, *The Southern Cross*, a staunch supporter of and source of inspiration for all the Adelaide Jocists, who in 1973 became YCS national chaplain; Brian Moylan and David Schinnick, who worked for the Christian Life Movement (CLM), a Jocist variant involving mainly married (of course) adults; and various YCW full-timers, including Julia Twohig, Meredith Evans, and Geoff Day and others. I learnt a great deal from all of these people, my network expanding yet further. Through frequent discussions with them I thought more about the 'review of life', which was also used by the YCW and CLM groups, gradually seeing it as the heart of the YCS activities. Even the gospel readings that were part of the meetings of all three movements were largely a source of inspiration for the review of life and 'doing good', as best we could, in the situations in which we found ourselves.

It was, of course, a tumultuous time for Australia, with growing opposition to the war in Vietnam and to conscription, seen as needed to provide the numbers of soldiers needed for the Australian role in the unjust Vietnam conflict, and increasing opposition to that role. I was well aware of the possibility of being conscripted, something that contributed to my taking an interest in the war, and I gradually formed a strong view that Australia's role in it was unjustified. I was also aware of growing concern that there was much else about how Australia operated that should be questioned.

When I decided to stay on in the YCS job for a second year (1971), I could not further defer my Commonwealth Scholarship, and so enrolled in part-time BA studies at Flinders University, taking up a year-long history course on five revolutions, including the Russian and the Chinese revolutions of the 20th century. The course was taught very well, and built an understanding for me of the roots of those revolutions being in large part in struggles against exploitation (of various kinds) and inequality. By the first part of 1970 I was keen to take part in the anti-apartheid demonstrations against the white South African Springbok rugby team tour planned for Adelaide in June of that year.

So new ideas I was exposed to, one way or another, and my widening network of Jocist colleagues from the late 1960s, were undoubtedly influencing the way I thought about the world. During 1970 this was already beginning to have an impact on how I approached the

YCS 'review of life'. It was gradually becoming more clear that there was a wider setting than just personal and school circumstances in which I, and other YCS members, could work to seek change. The increasing discussion that was going on amongst the expanding group of Australian YCS full-timers in 1970, and especially early 1971, the horizon for action to achieve positive change was, I think expanding for the YCS as a whole. For me, the real change in that regard came early in 1971.

4. Mark's work in the national team, 1971–1972

Three core activities soon consumed the days of work. First was the updating of old publications and writing of new materials to send out to the 300–400 registered groups across the country. There was a regular newsletter to populate with stories, key publications such as a booklet on group dynamics and another on the basic of leadership that were reviewed and given occasional new examples or recent news items to keep them current. The second was planning for key meetings such as the regular leadership training workshops and meetings of religious assistants—the nuns and priests who organised local groups at their schools or parishes. And the final and most important element of the job was called visitation. I later learned that the biblical notion of visitation is what is called a countable noun indicating an event in which god or another spiritual being appears or makes contact. Well, a big part of our role was to appear and make contact—but in our case it involved less spiritual mystery and a lot of driving.

Long road trips to far-flung places were the regular work of the team. We would travel in twos or threes and stay in a place for several days, usually being boarded with one of the local leaders' families. The idea was to refresh the local groups with new energy and pass along ideas for things they might consider. Usually this was informal work with small numbers of leaders and attendance at regular meetings to see how things were proceeding. Sometimes special training sessions would be organised to bring people from neighbouring areas. But it was also an informal advertisement for the student movement itself and we were often called upon to address a school assembly or take part in larger community events that aimed to improve understanding of 'the youth of today' and so on.

My first solo visitation was to Launceston in late 1971 where the movement had only a small base involving two or three groups. The big objective was to recruit more members. I was boarded at the local presbytery and among other tasks was asked to give the guest speech at an all-school assembly at the local high school. On a large stage with a powerful microphone I addressed 1200 students with the full teaching staff stacked in rows behind me. I cannot recall much about the content of the twenty minute address except for the fact that it may have involved quite a bit about Bob Dylan and not as much Jesus as the local curate was expecting. We had a lengthy debate about that back at the presbytery and he later introduced me to an excellent hang-over cure.

I recall this work with both amazement and amusement. We were encouraging young people to get organised and we had certain useful tools to help them, including ways to recruit people to groups, a methodology based on Cardijn's 'review of life' and a fair amount of enthusiasm to help build confidence among kids who had yet to experience their own leadership. These remain powerful accomplishments and I meet people even now, so many years later, who believe these experiences changed their lives. This was, and still is, amazing to me. And the amusing part was that all this took place in an atmosphere of cheerful egalitarianism where nothing was safe from a good joke or a levelling anecdote and everyone got their day in the sun.

But part way through 1971 this began to change. There was already a noticeable shift in the kinds of issues being discussed in local groups as the Red School Book issue was suggesting. The personal reflections and actions were broadening to include debates about the Vietnam War and about racism. Equality for women and their fair treatment was also part of the agenda some groups would raise. But the galvanising force for change was also external to us and as yet, barely recognised. Our colleagues in the YCW had already enjoyed a deep connection with a wider international workers movement and by 1970 this included the radicalising ideas of the South American liberation theologists and activists. Some of us were privy to these discussions but I think it's fair to say that the leading chaplains then involved in the student movement were not so aware, and if they were, many were hostile to these ideas.

5. A Singapore story: Anthony's perceptions

Early in 1971, the activities of the national (Melbourne) and Adelaide YCS offices converged into an intense engagement with the international YCS organisation (something that had, for me, hitherto attracted little more attention than an acknowledgment that it existed). The national team advised Australian diocesan YCS offices that Australian YCS had been invited to send a representative to an intensive leadership workshop for senior leaders of YCS movements in Southeast Asia, to be held in Singapore, in—I think—April, perhaps May, 1971. The National President, Sue Carman, had been chosen to attend to represent Australia. The national office also asked all diocesan offices to complete what I recall was a quite extensive questionnaire coming from the Singapore regional YCS office, asking us to identify and analyse major social and political issues facing our country.

I began working with others, both in the Adelaide YCS and amongst the Diocesan Building colleagues, to develop an Adelaide YCS response. I had a particularly long and intense discussion with Wilko, who in contributing ideas about national issues that should be included in the response was also clearly excited, I think now, by what he could see as a welcome change of direction in the YCS in the questions coming from Singapore. He told me that it was vital to have wider participation from Australia in what he saw as a meeting of significance for the Australian Jocist movements generally. Sue should not represent Australia alone, he insisted, and instead I should go as well.

As far as I can recall, the Adelaide YCS 'authorities' supported Wilko's proposal. There was no question, however, of the parlous Adelaide YCS finances meeting the costs of international fares, and instead Wilko very generously took it on himself to raise the necessary funds from contributions, mainly from those diocesan building Jocist colleagues. The funding was forthcoming remarkably promptly and the national office agreed that I could go to Singapore. Before my departure, Wilko made it clear to me that the financial contributions were in the nature of an investment by him and those diocesan building colleagues in what they saw as important new directions, of which he envisaged that they too would be a part.

So Sue and I set off for Singapore, the first overseas trip for either of us. There was a front page photo of us in that week's Southern Cross, showing us at the Adelaide airport, standing at the bottom of the steps for the flight for the first leg of our journey. Fifty-two years on, the details of what occurred at the workshop are no longer clear. It ran for at least two weeks of intense discussion, attended by twenty or thirty people, mainly student leaders, full-timers and priests and nuns assisting YCS groups. The focus was on expanding our appreciation of the Jocist 'review of life'. We discussed situations of political and economic injustice from the countries that participants came from, much of which was absolutely new to Sue and I, and to some extent shocking. There was a strong emphasis on looking beyond just the problem situations involved, and in addition making serious efforts to understand the causes of particular situations of injustice or inequality. Intense discussion about the issues included a focus on about how secondary and tertiary students could, realistically, become involved in action in relation to the causes and manifestations of the kinds of injustice and inequality being discussed. The gospel was not entirely forgotten, but drawn on mainly as a source of inspiration for efforts to better understand injustice and inequality with a view to pertinent action against it. The key person quietly pushing the discussion to new depth, through thoughtful and incisive questions and comments, was undoubtedly Southeast Asia full-timer, Johannes Lee (a Singaporean). A highly energetic and articulate Malaysian priest of Indian descent, whose nickname of 'Bala' is all I remember of his name, was also a key voice in challenging the participants.

The focus on injustice, and inequality and its causes, and on action in relation to causes, was largely a new way of thinking for me. At the same time, it helped me to synthesise previous ideas about 'doing good' with such things as criticism of Australian involvement in the Vietnam war and South Africa's apartheid regime, and to seek to analyse underlying causes as well as the impacts of a much wider range of injustice and inequality. Of course, such new approaches did not come together in a single step. I recall clearly a discussion, some days in to the workshop, during a break, when Johannes asked me about my plans when I finished working with the YCS, only a few months later. When I explained my interest in studying and working on industrial relations, he thought a minute, and said: 'When you understand the review of life, you won't want to do that'. Of course, he was right. Sue and I returned to Australia with a sense of mission, to bring more critical thinking to the YCS, through the way the review of life was conducted, and we found fertile ground for developing such ideas in the network of 'full-timers', and a few of the key chaplains and other advisers involved in the YCS.

As for me, the approach that the YCS was embracing in 1971 had long term and still-continuing influences, despite the Catholic Church and its doctrines and practices having long-since ceased to engage me. Those influences were manifest in a complete change in my choice of university course from 1972, in subsequent career and employment choices, and in the way in which I work and the things in relation to which I do work, still in 2023. It has also in many ways shaped the networks of colleagues of various kinds that I have maintained and continue to develop.

6. The Singapore story: Mark's perception

When Sue and Anthony returned a crystallising of new approaches took place across the senior members of the movement. It is difficult with this much distance to be precise about exactly how this shift played out, but I do recall just how ready we seemed to be, and then how quickly we embraced the idea that social action and concerted work to bring about social change should become important to our focus.

Part of this shift in direction also involved a change of personnel. Fr Kane was a much-admired chaplain of the old school who had been in the role a long time and it was the right moment for him to go back to his job as a parish priest. But negotiations for a replacement proved difficult. No work had been done to groom his successor and some of the best advisers available to us at the time were nuns, not priests. This raised other issues for the bishops at a time when we were asking a lot of them. Negotiations stalled.

Adding complexity to the transition was the fact that Sue was due to finish her term and wished to step down from the team, as did Liz Whitehouse. On the positive side, a very accomplished leader from the Canberra movement, Anne Keogh, had agreed to take a full-time role. But even so, this reduced the national team to a national couple, as many were want to point out. So we would go into 1972 with a major new change agenda, no chaplain, and only two national full time workers. But help was at hand.

One of the very practical outcomes of the Singapore meeting was an agreement to host South East Asia fulltime worker, Johannes Lee for an extended Australian visit. As 1972 was also the year for the biennial national conference, we planned for him to come in May so he could participate in the preparations and then make a contribution to the conference itself. A second string to our bow was to make greater use of Trevor Bate as part of the national team and to include Melbourne full timer, Carmel Brown as part of the group planning the new national agenda. Tricia Mitchell and Jan Allen were also working fulltime in Wagga and Adelaide respectively and Wendy Foley in Brisbane had also become a key player in shaping the new work from Brisbane. Anthony remained a key mentor, always positive about the road ahead and brilliant at seeing the wide picture forming around us.

The conference was held in Canberra at one of the residential colleges at the ANU and there was spirited discussion and some debate about the direction we were taking. A few of the priests were concerned that their traditional roles were being reduced and the chaplain from Wagga, Fr Vince Kiss, used one of the open forum sessions of the conference to question the role of a national team that did not have a proper spiritual adviser to direct the lay members correctly. Happily we had previously arranged with the bishops that Fr Tom Doyle would be our advisor in such matters and although he was not at the conference he provided a deflection for some of the concerns being expressed. But tensions concerning the premier role of the clergy would persist. The relationship was changing. I think looking back this was not so much a rejection of the notion of priesthood by some of the new leaders, as a greater willingness to question and to try and align some idea of shared leadership of the things traditionally reserved to priests in the old church.

At a meeting with Melbourne priests and nuns later that year I recall facing strong questioning about the apparently radical turn the movement seemed to be taking. But equally memorable was the willing enthusiasm of a number of nuns at that meeting who saw this as a vindication of the Vatican II message to take the Church into the world and as one of them put it, 'to leave behind the idea that the Church is a place of sanctuary for the virtuous to hide from a world of sin'.

The themes of the conference echoed the broader desire to allow young people a say in the future of their societies, both local and national. Johannes gave inspiring examples of groups tackling issues of poverty and discrimination and making significant contributions to a more just and peaceful world. He had a quiet confidence that was infectious and practical and his influence lived on long after his visit. He helped cement the idea that the student movement was a real player in social life and the YCS could be a key part of that movement.

To drive home the themes of the conference we then set ourselves an ambitious visitation agenda. Trev and I would travel to all the key cities along the east coast as far as Cairns, while Anne and Carmel would cover everything west of Melbourne to Perth and Geraldton. It was an exhausting three months but it gave us a chance to set-out the ideals of the movement as a force for change and an account of leadership that included personal development but also went beyond that to include skills in social analysis and organisation. We had embraced the idea that the Kingdom of God was not a separate realm in the afterlife but a practical community to be built right here, right now.

We ended the year with exciting new appointments to the national team. Trev and I would be leaving to start university. Three new full timers would join Anne in the national team—Michael Perkins, Kevin McDonald and Roger Slee. And in keeping with the temper of the times, I recall one last heated argument with the bishops as they learned we had appointed a non-Catholic to a full-time role. Roger was the best person for the job but we were also pushing the limits, no doubt.

As we know, the late 1960s and early 1970s saw a remarkable upsurge in social movements around the world and Australia was no exception. It was not merely that 'the times were a changing', but also that young people were intent on changing them. We took our place in that transformation and in the process we became different people. This meant that the YCS had to find new ways to work and different methods for supporting the aspirations of students, a process that continues to this day.

Conclusion

As we both handed our leadership roles over to others and embraced a new life at university the future of the movement felt positive, although it was certain that new ways of working might also mean a different mode of action at the local level. It was not clear whether the older model involving large numbers of groups and a more individual approach to action would always translate well into a new invitation to consider bigger social issues and struggles. But for the leadership at least, the transformative power of the work would continue and the challenge to connect with the international perspectives of worker and student movements would continue to shape our future.

Biographical Details on the Contributors

Linda Baker, was born and raised in Perth, Western Australia and attended the Mercedes School for Girls. She studied arts at the University of WA and theology at Flinders University via St Frances Xavier Seminary in Adelaide. During her university years, Linda was heavily involved in student politics, and was the Australian Union of Students (AUS) state organiser for Western Australia. Working for four years for the YCS both in Perth and Nationally, she became YCS National President in 1980. In the early 1980's she wrote a series of articles based on Cardijn teachings and the YCS for The Record, the Catholic newspaper in Perth, and these articles have been reprinted elsewhere over the years. Moving to Adelaide in 1983 she was appointed Youth Minister at Hectorville Parish followed by being the Electorate Officer for Norwood for The Honourable Greg Crafter. Norwood was previously held by Don Dunstan. It was the YCW/YCS connection that led Linda to meet Greg Crafter. In the early 2,000's Linda decided to move into the real estate industry, and has held several positions in sales, sales management and now is a partner in Barry Plant Norwood. It is the first Barry Plant franchise in South Australia. Linda has achieved several Real Estate Institute of South Australia (REISA) awards, and has been a finalist in the inaugural Real Estate Business Women's National Awards. Linda has sat on the Real Estate Employer's Federation (REEF) Board for South Australia and the Northern Territory, and currently sits on the board for the Real Estate Employers Federation (REEF) Australia and holds the position of Vice President of REEF Australia.

Trevor Bate, after working for YCS in 1970–1971 and some initial study, Trevor worked in various jobs until further study led to a career in information technology. For forty years, Trevor worked in the development, implementation, support and management of complex IT systems, ending as a project manager before retiring in 2021. He has been an active member of the Catholic parishes of Woodville and Henley Beach and has been involved in Adelaide diocesan activities. Trevor is currently one of the mentors for Adelaide YCW. Trevor is married with three grown children and six growing grandchildren.

Carmel Brown's YCS experience commenced as a 1965 year-6 schooler in a northern Melbourne parish junior girls' YCS group. It took various forms over a fourteen-year period which also included school-based membership, participation in various national structures, and employment with Melbourne YCS and national Tertiary YCS—the latter in 1979 and 1980. Between then and now, she has had periods of close contact with several YCS friends. Carmel has taught in schools, TAFE and university; and policy in education and criminal justice –a roundabout of policy and practice.

Mark Considine is Redmond Barry Distinguished Professor of Political Science at the University of Melbourne. He is a Fellow of the Academy of Social Sciences of Australia and a Fellow of the Institute of Public Administration of Australia. He served as the Provost of the University of Melbourne between 2017 and 2020. In this role, he was Chief Academic Officer of the University and Standing Deputy to the Vice Chancellor and helped lead the University's response to the pandemic. From 2007 to 2017, he was Dean of the Faculty of Arts and with his team undertook a comprehensive program of academic and organisational reform.

Brian Lawrence was a fulltime worker for the Australian YCS, holding the positions of National Secretary in 1968 and National President in 1969. He was a barrister from 1971 until 2008, during which time he held appointments as Deputy President of the Industrial Relations Commission of Victoria and Chairman of the Police Service Board of Victoria. In 1972 Brian married Elizabeth Proust, a fellow fulltime worker for the YCS in 1969. Elizabeth has held a number of senior government and corporate positions since the 1980s and was Deputy Chair of the Church's Truth Justice and Healing Council. Brian was the honorary chairman of the Australian Catholic Council for Employment Relations, an agency of the Australian Catholic Bishops Conference, from 2007 to 2015. From 2003 to 2019 he prepared and presented submissions on behalf of the Church in the annual national minimum wage cases, based on the premise that the wages system must provide a decent standard of living for low paid workers and working families. In 2015 he was awarded a papal knighthood (KSS) for this advocacy. His continuing special interest is the content and application of Catholic Social Teaching. Since 2016 he has been a member of the College of Consultors of Catholic Mission and since 2020 he has been President of the Australian Cardijn Institute.

Anthony J Regan worked as a YCS 'full-timer' in Adelaide, South Australia, 1970–1971, and then studied law 1972–1975. After working as a lawyer for five years in Adelaide, in 1981 he began working as a lawyer in Papua New Guinea's Department of Decentralisation, the first of a series of jobs involving implementing peace settlements through new constitutional arrangements. He is now a professor (constitutional law and peace-building) in the Department of Pacific Affairs at The Australian National University. He has been actively involved in several conflict resolution processes (including Bougainville/PNG, Solomon Islands, Sri Lanka, and the Naga areas of NE India), and in several post-conflict constitution-making processes (including Uganda, Bougainville, Fiji, Solomon Islands, and Timor L'Este). Usually accompanied by his family, he has lived and worked for extended periods in Papua New Guinea (fifteen years), Uganda (over three years) and Bougainville (three years).

Pat Walsh was active in the YCS 1968–1978, as a chaplain in the Ballarat diocese then as national chaplain. He spent the rest of his working life promoting international human rights, particularly self-determination and reconciliation in East Timor.

Cathy Whewell was a member of the YCS throughout her time at high school. After a year on the YCS Diocesan Committee Cathy worked for the YCS in the Archdiocese of Adelaide. Her tenure was for a two year from 1974–1975. After YCS, Cathy was part of forming the Tertiary YCS that brought tertiary students together nationally. In 1978 Cathy was part of the Australian delegation attending the World Council of the YCS in Valladolid, Spain. Since the YCS Cathy has lived out the gifts received from the YCS in her life and work in the Catholic Church in a wide variety of positions. More recently she has worked as a leadership coach specialising in social and emotional intelligence and leadership. Cathy is committed to creative and productive ways of working with conflict and is a trained Mediator.

Ingram Content Group UK Ltd.
Milton Keynes UK
UKHW010230170623
423577UK00007B/685